# SOUTH AFRICA:

## CHALLENGE AND HOPE

by the
Southern Africa Working Party
of the
AMERICAN FRIENDS SERVICE COMMITTEE

Published by
American Friends Service Committee
in cooperation with
African Studies Program
Indiana University

1982

At its meeting on April 24, 1982, the Board of
Directors of the American Friends Service Committee
accepted this report prepared for its consideration,
and warmly endorsed it as a statement of the
Board's own views.

Published by
American Friends Service Committee
1501 Cherry Street, Philadelphia, Pa. 19102
In cooperation with
African Studies Program, Indiana University
Bloomington, Indiana 47405

Library of Congress Catalog Card Number: 82-72895
ISBN: 0-910082-03-0

# CONTENTS

# BIOGRAPHICAL NOTES

## AFSC Southern Africa Working Party Members

### HARRY AMANA
Journalism lecturer at the University of North Carolina in Chapel Hill; member of AFSC International Division Executive Committee; member AFSC Information-Interpretation Committee; former staff member of AFSC Third World Coalition; member AFSC study tour to Frontline States in 1977.

### MARY B. ANDERSON
Development economist with special interest in Asia and Africa, particularly in rural development, self-reliance and indigenous technology development; AFSC volunteer in Tanzania, 1951–63; education program staff in Chicago region for six years; director of Program Resources for Midwest Regional Office two years; member of the Middle East Panel; member of the Program Priorities Committee for New England Regional Office and of New England Regional Office Executive Committee.

### VINCENT HARDING
Born in Harlem; holds degree in journalism and a doctorate in history; deeply active in civil rights struggle in the south; history professor; Director of the Martin Luther King Center and of the Institute of the Black World in Atlanta; formerly on the faculty of Pendle Hill; Professor of Religion and Social Transformation at Iliff Seminary; author of *There is a River, the Black Struggle for Freedom.*

### LEWIS HOSKINS
Formal education in history; several staff assignments with the AFSC, 1945–59, including the position of AFSC Executive Secretary 1951–59; has made about 15 visits to Africa, mainly South Africa and Kenya; Vice Chairman, U.S.–South Africa Leader Exchange Program; AFSC Board member; Professor Emeritus of History, Earlham College.

### ANN STEVER
Active with AFSC in Pacific Northwest Region since 1965 including Chair of the Regional Executive Committee and concentration in work relating to employment discrimination, the criminal justice system, desegregation of public schools and Native American treaty rights; National Board of Directors, 1972–78, and beginning a new term in 1981; Vice-Chair of Board, 1975–78; member of AFSC Study Tour to the Frontline States, August 1977; Clerk of AFSC Delegation to the area of Southern Africa Yearly Meeting, August 1980.

## LYLE TATUM
Longtime AFSC relationships including AFSC representative in Southern Rhodesia, 1960–64, and Secretary of the Peace Education Division, 1972–75; observed Zimbabwe talks in Geneva in 1976 and London in 1979 as AFSC representative; part of AFSC Zimbabwe Transition Team, January–April, 1980; Clerk, AFSC International Division Africa Panel; Clerk, Southern Africa Committee of Philadelphia Yearly Meeting.

## C. H. MIKE YARROW
Education and teaching in government, political theory, international law; work with AFSC, 1952–72, the last ten years as Secretary of International Affairs Division, active in the U.S. civil rights movement; brief visits to west Africa, east Africa, and Salisbury; member AFSC Board of Directors; author of *Quaker Experiences in International Conciliation.*

## *Staff Consultants*

## JERRY HERMAN
Interpersonal communications specialist; formerly an instructor at Southern Illinois University; civil rights activist and former AFSC Program Chairperson in St. Louis; has travelled widely in north and West Africa; spent time studying and filming the Dogon Cliff dwellers of Mali; member AFSC delegation to South Africa, 1980; presently National Coordinator for AFSC's Peace Education Southern Africa Program.

## MAGHAN KEITA
Africanist specializing in political economy, history and development with emphasis on southern Africa; research in urban and rural areas of West and North Africa; currently a member of the Africa Desk of the International Division of AFSC with responsibility for southern Africa and the Horn of Africa.

## JOHN A. SULLIVAN
AFSC Associate Executive Secretary for Information and Interpretation, retired 1982; former AFSC Regional Executive Secretary; extensive news media experience before AFSC period of service.

## BILL SUTHERLAND
Civil rights activist; conscientious objector and imprisoned during World War II; nonviolence activist; co-founder of the American Committee on Africa; worked in Ghana, 1953–60; Tanzania, 1961–74; AFSC Southern Africa Representative, 1974–81.

# CHAPTER 1

# *Introduction*

Freedom is the theme of this book, specifically, the heroic struggle for freedom in South Africa. The particular meaning of freedom for South Africa must be worked out by its own people, but others who care about freedom and recognize the commonality of human experience may not simply leave South Africa to South Africa. As the Information Counselor of the South African Embassy in Washington, D.C. wrote, South Africa represents "the world in microcosm." ("A World in Microcosm," *Backgrounder,* No. 6/80, July 1980) Within South Africa, he argues, is a "human mosaic" representing a variety of cultures and ethnic backgrounds, even as in the world.

The world is also reflected in the political and economic structures of South African society, in which a white, wealthy and westernized minority exercises and maintains dominance over a black majority through military force. Today the northern industrialized world feels pressure from the nations of Africa, Asia and Latin America as they seek their rightful share of the world's wealth and power. Just as the Afrikaners and English speaking groups of South Africa do not know how to respond to the demands of the black in their country,* these northern nations do not know how to respond to this more global pressure. While this conflict occurs in South Africa, all of us in the human family are linked in the struggle to maintain or to share power.

Thus, inside and outside South Africa people seek to understand the obstacles to freedom which have developed there and the extent to which their own actions contribute to sustaining or removing these obstacles. As a

---

*In this context, "black" includes those called African, coloured and Asian. The term "non-white," formerly applied to this group, is no longer acceptable to blacks, as it defines them by what they are not, as well as using white for the frame of reference. As an indication of the unity of the oppressed, these three groups all wish to be known collectively as blacks. There is confusion, however, as in South Africa "black" is often used to mean only those most of the world calls African. In this book, black will be used only as a collective term for Africans, coloured and Asians.

microcosm of our own experience, South Africa presents a challenge and a hope to all of us. This study addresses that challenge and hope.

## Working Party Approach

In September 1979 the Board of Directors of the American Friends Service Committee convened a group of volunteers and staff who had had experience in southern Africa to carry out an intensive study of the human, political and economic situation there and to suggest ways in which everyone might work to end the inhumanity of the system of apartheid. This task was not undertaken lightly.

In addressing the racism of apartheid in South Africa, we do not pose as citizens of a country whose human problems have been solved. As U.S. citizens, we acknowledge our own history of conquest of the American Indian homeland and the slaughter of Native Americans by Europeans pushing relentlessly into the interior of the continent. We remember the nightmare of our Civil War, the lynchings and the slavery. And we are painfully conscious of the current manifestations of that  inhumanity, the present realities of *de facto* segregation, economic injustice, discrimination and of our failure to secure the political and social rights of those Native Americans and people of African, Asian and Hispanic origin in the United States.

The fundamental issues of race, class and gender are still unsettled among us, and the AFSC continues to address these issues in its domestic programs.

In South African terms we are outsiders, but our lives are significantly touched by what happens in South Africa. We know that U.S. experience has an effect on racism there. When there have been victories against racism in the U.S., these have been welcomed in black Africa and when there are setbacks in our country, both white and black Africa have taken note. Our racially mixed citizenry is alert to and sensitive to racial developments in other countries. The United States is a powerful country with interests and influence in South Africa—industrial, commercial and political. Few Americans are not beneficiaries of commerce and investments related to South Africa—as businesspeople, investors or simply holders of bank accounts or retirement benefits.

Even as we are struggling with racial problems in the United States, we are also involved in the racial situation of South Africa. Thus, if women and men can find a truly human response and solution to the problems of South Africa, these will offer a challenge, hope, and example to the rest of the world.

The Old Testament prophet Micah envisioned a world in which all people might "live in peace and unafraid." The tragedy of domination, of one group of people holding power over others, is that such a situation produces fear, a fear that distorts their lives and their children's lives.

As we look at South Africa we see both fear and anger marking the relationships among racial groups, and we see that no group is free from this fear. What are people in South Africa afraid of?

> If I am black in South Africa, I am afraid, daily, that I can be sent away from my home, my family, my place of work. I fear for my children's education. I fear becoming a noncitizen of my country which is declared not to be my country, with unknown loss of rights for myself and even more certainly for my children. I fear I will be exiled to places of worklessness and poverty and underdevelopment, places with which I feel no affinity and have no associations, so that my family has to separate to survive. What have I done to deserve this? Why must I be pushed out as if I had never been educated, to battle like an animal for survival, while the whites appropriate all the wealth blacks have developed and the cities we have built? I fear white control. But I am not only afraid. I am angry, very angry. Because even those white people who profess religion and have the vote and a voice in Parliament, never raise it for me, never use their power, privilege or money to identify with me in my struggle for freedom and justice, or to change the system. We know the whites know this. We know they are afraid of black anger and hopes because they own everything. So I am afraid of my helplessness in the face of arbitrary political decisions made by others about me. I am afraid of arrest and imprisonment. I fear the fear that whites feel. I am afraid of white people.

> If I am white in South Africa, I am afraid of forces I do not understand: forces which may take from me the things to which I have become accustomed. I am afraid of a future born of a past for which I am held accountable, circumstances which I inherited but which the world tells me are wrong. I am afraid of a hostile world which tells me that I must change and which does not understand my plight. I fear the loss of my own privilege and wealth which set me apart from the mass of my country's people and seems to identify me as a target. I am afraid that I may become helpless in the face of arbitrary political decisions made by others about me. I fear the fear and anger that black people feel. I am afraid of black people.

Knowing that freedom, peace or justice cannot be achieved on the basis of fear, the American Friends Service Committee has undertaken this study in keeping with its efforts of more than sixty years toward a peaceful and just world. The AFSC has long been concerned with the problems of southern Africa. One of the founders of the AFSC, Rufus Jones, and his wife Elizabeth travelled to South Africa in 1938 at the invitation of South African Friends (Quakers), beginning a relationship which has continued to the present day. In the intervening years, the AFSC has sponsored or assisted efforts in leadership development, humanitarian service and support for self-determination in South Africa and the other southern Africa countries. Because this work has provided an important background to the effort of this study, we shall trace some of its more significant aspects here. It should be useful not only to report on the areas of AFSC involvement in southern Africa, but also to highlight for our purpose here the dilemmas and difficulties encountered in those efforts.

### U.S.-South Africa Leader Exchange Program

In 1956 at Haverford College a conference was held which had its origin in a concern for greater communication between the United States and South Africa. This conference grew out of visits to South African Friends by leading American Quakers, among them Douglas and Dorothy Steere of Haverford, Pennsylvania, and the late Frank Loescher of Philadelphia. It brought together representatives of churches, foundations, universities and colleges, and included an observer from the U.S. Department of State. The participants concluded that a program of private exchanges between U.S. citizens and South Africans could facilitate a badly needed growth of understanding between the two peoples.

The United States–South Africa Leader Exchange Program (USSALEP) was created with Frank Loescher as General Secretary. A binational board of managers included representatives from various ethnic groups from both countries. USSALEP accepted no funding from either government, relying instead on support from foundations, churches and private and business organizations. Participants in the exchanges were chosen from all ethnic groups and from many professions. This program has sponsored several hundred exchanges between the U.S. and South Africa, and is still continuing.

Over the years some special groups have been identified to increase the impact of these exchanges. Nearly twenty South African journalists have spent a year in the Nieman journalism program at Harvard University. More than two hundred teachers of science in South Africa have studied on American campuses in the summer programs of the National Science Institute. U.S. medical and scientific specialists have consulted with their professional counterparts in South Africa. Teams of academics, educational administrators and legal experts have visited the two countries.

Breaking traditional social barriers, the governing committee has sponsored interracial and international conferences in the U.S., South Africa and Europe. On a small but important scale, U.S. and South African professionals and leaders have discovered new perspectives on each other's society.

Private organizations such as USSALEP cannot escape moral dilemmas and problems in addressing the issues surrounding South Africa. How can programs appear reasonable to militant blacks and at the same time to conservative whites in both the U.S. and South Africa? Funds must be raised, but some of those most available may be tainted with special or partisan involvement. Programs that seem political to one group may seem humanitarian to another. For example, can Americans support individuals working within South Africa's homelands system when they oppose the entire homelands policy? How does an organization work for rapid social change within a restrictive atmosphere without at the same time condoning or buttressing the system it cannot support? How can a program train leaders in a divided society and at the same time help them avoid cooptation by a system they seek to change? These are central dilemmas to any outside organization which attempts to work in a country where the goal is fundamental change in that country's social and political structure.

## AFSC Representatives in Southern Africa

In 1957 the AFSC sent the first of two couples as its representatives to southern Africa. George and Eleanor Loft were based in Southern Rhodesia, now Zimbabwe. They were replaced in 1960 by Lyle and Elizabeth Tatum who were stationed in Salisbury for four years, travelling to South Africa, Kenya and Tanzania (then Tanganyika). In that period the political and economic power in the Central Africa Federation of Southern Rhodesia, Northern Rhodesia and Nyasaland (now Zimbabwe, Zambia and Malawi) were held entirely by white people, collectively called Europeans. The whites in Nyasaland and Northern Rhodesia accounted for less than 1 per cent of the population and 5 per cent in Southern Rhodesia. Society was highly segregated racially, but the British government and local white political leaders instituted the idea of racial partnership in the new Federation. African political leaders saw the Federation as a tool for maintaining white domination.

The AFSC representatives saw the difficulties in the racial partnership plans and developed programs to ease racial tensions and to find other terms for political power sharing. The homes of the Lofts and the Tatums served as nonracial meeting places for Africans, Asians and Europeans. Black, brown and white children in segregated schools in Rhodesia exchanged work with schools in the U.S. under the AFSC's School Affiliation Service (no longer operating). Gatherings of these children in Southern Rhodesia provided one of the few opportunities for them to meet and work together interracially.

As the political tensions in the area grew, George Loft began visiting African leaders in jail and detention, and Lyle Tatum continued the practice. Some of those former detainees are now heads of African governments or leaders of African liberation movements.

The heritage of the Lofts' and Tatums' work was the establishment of a good relationship between the American Quaker representatives and African political leaders along with some European leaders. This rapport later allowed British and American Quakers to be active in support of a political settlement in Zimbabwe. Quaker representatives were unofficial observers at the Geneva Conference on Zimbabwe in 1976 and in the London Lancaster House Conference ending with an actual settlement in 1979.

The Zimbabwe experience deepened AFSC's presence in southern Africa and revealed certain continuing dilemmas as well as some factors supporting positive change. African suspicions and low expectations for change as well as white supremacy views obstructed progress for many years. An outside organization has a limited role to play in effecting change. But a small effort sustained over several years can support the work of others in meaningful ways. AFSC staff members frequently violated certain regulations and customs: visiting friends' homes in African townships restricted to whites, entertaining friends regardless of race in their own homes (resulting in eviction by one landlord), and visiting prisoners branded "terrorists" or "revolutionaries" at the time. Lyle Tatum was declared a prohibited immigrant by Southern Rhodesia in 1964 and not allowed to reenter the country until after the Lancaster House Agreement fifteen years later.

These experiences raise issues for AFSC workers. How can one do what seems to be morally required and keep one's integrity while still trying to maintain avenues of communication with all segments of a divided society? How does one balance the importance of witnessing to fundamental beliefs with the desire to be effective in realistic political terms? These questions continue as the AFSC probes for ways of appropriate involvement in Namibia and South Africa.

### Zambia and Nonviolence

AFSC service programs began in Zambia in 1964, focusing on self-help housing, community development and agricultural development. The AFSC program continues today in Zambia, but is in the process of being transferred to a local organization.

At the express invitation of President Kenneth Kaunda in 1965 James and Dorothy Bristol were sent by AFSC to Zambia where they remained until 1967. Kaunda proposed that the AFSC see how nonviolence might be relevant in the developing life of the new nation (founded October 14, 1964). He had led Zambia to independence by nonviolent methods. A devout Christian influenced by the example of Mahatma Gandhi, whose portrait hung on his office wall, Kaunda told his inner circle of colleagues more than once during the liberation struggle that if they felt they must use violence he would step down as their leader for independence.

James Bristol was in close touch with the President until November 11,

1965, the date of the unilateral Declaration of Independence (UDI) of white-led Southern Rhodesia. The results of UDI were catastrophic for Zambia, and Kaunda became fully preoccupied with its economic, political and ideological consequences, some of which challenged his faith in nonviolence.

Unlike the United States, England, Western Europe and India, Zambia had no group of people dedicated to the theory and practice of nonviolence. Kenneth Kaunda was virtually alone in this commitment, so that when he was diverted by the impact of UDI, there was no other local Zambian base. So the Bristols began to improvise a program. They opened their home to people of all races, promoted discussions, launched a weekly luncheon meeting and tried to think of nonviolent approaches to the UDI situation in Rhodesia. They built up many contacts with liberation movement people, especially from Zimbabwe, Namibia and South Africa. Some of these visited the Bristols frequently, fully aware of their pacifism. There were searching discussions of nonviolence and its relevance to the struggle for freedom.

Two developments were notable:

Five liberation organizations were enabled to meet consistently with European and American visitors and to explain their aims firsthand. These talks were important for correcting misapprehensions about liberation leadership and motivations in the eyes of Europeans and North Americans and also for challenging movement members to acknowledge their larger international context, their support from abroad and their responsibility for finding political alternatives as they sought freedom for their people.

Bristol and some of the people of the Namibian liberation movement explored the idea of a nonviolent action to move into Walvis Bay in Namibia in 1966 and take it over for the Namibian people. Upon his return to the U.S. Bristol talked with British and American Quakers and specialists on Africa, and the "sail-in" idea was implemented as a "fly-in." In the fall of 1967 two light planes flew to Namibia. Refused a landing at Windhoek by South African police, they were forced to fly on to Botswana, landing with empty fuel tanks. This action was enthusiastically received by the government and citizens of Zambia where the flight began.

### The Liberation Movements

Bill Sutherland, an AFSC representative committed to nonviolence and a veteran of years of work in Ghana and Tanzania, was appointed by AFSC in 1974 to relate directly to the southern African liberation movements. His job was to spend long periods of time in Africa with people involved in these movements, lending what support he could, and to return periodically to the United States to share his knowledge with government, business, universities and the press as well as with the growing movement of black and white citizens who were becoming active against South Africa's system of apartheid. He also was to explore the extent of U.S. involvement in and responsibility for the continuation of white rule in southern Africa.

While Sutherland maintained contact at high levels of government and in liberation movements, he also continued his AFSC service work. He provided direct humanitarian assistance, helping families survive, furnishing medicines and clothing and visiting prisoners in jail. He felt the importance of relating directly to human suffering in the struggle for self-determination and decried the way in which engagement in ideological conflict can obscure the plight of people.

In his years as Southern African Representative for the AFSC Sutherland, in both direct conversation and correspondence, repeatedly proposed nonviolent alternative methods of struggle with such African leaders as Kaunda of Zambia, Nyerere of Tanzania, Mugabe of Zimbabwe and Nujoma of Namibia. Known as a person committed to nonviolence and coming in the succession of AFSC representatives, he was accepted on the terms of his own principled position. He was asked for aid in ways that did not violate these principles, because his (and AFSC's) position was understood and respected.

Both Bristol's and Sutherland's experiments with nonviolence raised dilemmas for the AFSC. People suffering oppression will always seek freedom by either violent or nonviolent means, or a combination of both, and it is fruitless, perhaps irrelevant, to advise them to choose only nonviolent means. It is crucial to perceive what grinding poverty, hunger, unemployment, lack of educational opportunity, discrimination and apartheid mean, not only to those who suffer under them but also to those who take up the struggle for their freedom. It is crucial to realize the dehumanization that enforcing oppression causes the oppressors. There is a violence of the status quo in oppressive situations which must be opposed with no less vigor than the violence of war. There is also the violence of "law and order"—unjust laws, the pass system, police raids at night, the disappearances of people, the shooting of children, detention without charge. Where these forms of violence exist it is impossible to be neutral because of the clear wrong being done by one group to another. The dilemma is how to continue to work with both sides and to be heard by both.

As Bill Sutherland noted, nonviolent efforts have been underway in Africa for a great many years. Kaunda's and Nyerere's liberation struggles provide clear examples. In South Africa itself many campaigns based on nonviolence have been waged for decades, most notably the Defiance of Unjust Laws campaign (see Chapter 4). Kwame Nkrumah of Ghana brought the late A. J. Muste and other world pacifists to Africa in 1960 to seek nonviolent answers for African liberation. There is, across Africa, a history of commitment to and reliance on nonviolence in the struggles for freedom.

As AFSC work unfolded in Africa, it became critical for AFSC to help U.S. citizens understand the situation there and become motivated to push for U.S. withdrawal of support from apartheid and other systematic suppression of majorities in South Africa, Namibia and, at the time, Rhodesia. In 1973 James Bristol began an educational program in the U.S., focused on southern Africa, working to heighten the consciousness of U.S. citizens of events in Africa. The home visits of Bill Sutherland from the field were marked by speaking tours and consultations with white and black Americans across the continent. A full program on southern Africa was launched in October 1976 with Bristol as its first director, and it continues today, headed by Jerry Herman.

One of the first goals of this program was to expand the already existing movement to convince the U.S. government, banks and corporations to withdraw political and economic support from the white minority regimes in southern Africa. In June 1978 the AFSC Board of Directors decided to divest itself of all holdings in U.S. corporations that were doing business with or in South Africa.

As the domestic Southern African Program of AFSC got underway with broad educational efforts on injustice in South Africa, tensions grew between Quakers in South Africa and the United States. A series of visits and exchanges between South African and U.S. Friends was begun by the Friends World Committee for Consultation with AFSC assistance. The initial misunderstanding has diminished as those on both continents have come to see the differences in their approaches and the similarities of their concerns. These exchanges have contributed much to this study, deepening AFSC's understanding of the dilemmas faced daily by black and white South African Friends and the traumas and challenges they encounter at the human level regardless of race.

The full story of Quaker work in southern Africa would certainly include reports on the extensive involvement of British, South African and other Friends. This review has been confined to the work of AFSC over the years and has not attempted to describe the important work of other Quaker groups. Because this is an AFSC publication, we report some of our southern Africa involvement below.

The extensive contact of AFSC with southern Africa over the past twenty-five years has heightened the concern of the Board of Directors, committees, staff and constituency. The present study has been encouraged and supported by all these groups as we all seek directions for our own involvement in the inevitable and necessary transformation of South African society. Members of the Working Party who wrote this document have met together for over two years to study, consider and discuss the issues here presented. We have talked with leaders of African governments and liberation movements, with officials of the South African government and of the U.S. State Department and with academics, church people and others concerned with and knowledgeable about South Africa. A number of our members have lived and worked in southern Africa and half of our group have visited South Africa and South African Friends, black and white.

Writing was shared by the Working Party members. Every chapter was subjected to vigorous group review before and after rewriting. Before final approval, a draft copy of the study was circulated widely for criticism and suggestions in this country and overseas, including South Africa, among both whites and blacks.

The result, *South Africa: Challenge and Hope,* was approved by the AFSC Board of Directors at its meeting in Philadelphia in April 1982.

Chapter 2 presents the many facets of the system of apartheid, attempting to convey a sense of its pervasiveness and of what it means to live under that harsh system. The historical development of the current South African system is traced in Chapter 3. Chapter 4 tells the often untold story of black South African resistance to the growing power of the state over many years in the past and as it continues today. Chapters 5 and 6 discuss the inter-relationships, political and economic, of South Africa with the rest of the world and with international organizations. The potential of these relationships for supporting positive change in South Africa is also explored in Chapter 6. In Chapter 7 we struggle with the relevance of nonviolence to the status quo in South Africa, and we look for new and uncharted ways to discover new depths of commitment and experience in peaceful social change and the creation of just societies. In the final chapter we propose actions for moving toward a free South Africa, some focused on U.S. government initiatives, some for the U.S. public, and some for South Africa's government and people.

We believe that the problems of South Africa, like the problems of the United States, are at base spiritual, having to do with our sense of relationship to the divine, to the world around us, to our fellow beings and to our central basic beliefs. We believe that what people do politically is or ought to be an extension of the morality they profess. The spiritual ills of South Africa and of the United States are mirrored in the political realities of those countries. The moral responses to those realities will necessarily include action of a political nature.

# CHAPTER 2

# *Apartheid*

> South Africa is unqiue in building distinction according to race
> into the foundations of its political arrangements. Under the
> direction of skillful politicians and a ruthless security system, the
> fruit of this system has been cruelty and deprivation as profound
> as any known in this century.
>
> *Political Change in South Africa: Britain's Responsibility,*
> British Council of Churches, 1979, p. 2.

Apartheid is South Africa's sophisticated economic, political and social
system based on race. It is buttressed by a complex legal structure, security
system and theology that consolidates South Africa's wealth, power and
privilege in the hands of a white minority. Its social impact makes apartheid
one of the most pervasive and oppressive systems the world has known
because of its ability to disfigure humans spiritually as well as physically,
the oppressors as well as the oppressed. In a land of the vastness, beauty
and bounty of South Africa, apartheid is a tragedy that is twisting, maiming
and destroying the lives of its citizens, both black and white.

The tragedy can be expressed in a simple ratio of 87 to 13.* Four and one-
half million whites own 87% of the land, and twenty-two million Africans
are assigned to 13% of the land. This 13% is incapable of sustaining even
subsistence agriculture under present economic and political circumstances.

—or a ratio of 10 to 1, which describes the per capita allocation of
government funds for education of white and African students respectively
in 1980.

—or 13 to 1, which represents the rate of African infant mortality as opposed to that of whites, according to statistics of the South African Institute
of Race Relations: the number of infant deaths per 1000 live births was 12
for whites, 64 for urban Africans and 240 for rural Africans. Fifty per cent

---

*Precise estimates may vary depending on source and timing. For example, recent official
South African government statistics indicate that 13.7% of the land is now allocated to
Africans as a result of recent land transfers to the so-called independent states. At the same
time, however, Africans are relocated from lands so that precise allocations are in flux. We
make this point in such detail to illustrate a continuing problem with all figures in this document. In any situation when political divisions are deep, the choice of figures reflects political
biases. We have in each case considered the range of available figures and used those which
seem most credible to us.

of African deaths are of children under the age of five, according to a study of the South African Medical Research Council.

The apartheid system enmeshes all South Africans in a complex, interlocking web of restrictions which control and limit all aspects of life. In human terms, for most Africans it means poverty, malnutrition, threat of imprisonment, violence, crime, poor housing and separated families. It means the risk of freedom and life for those who challenge, oppose or try to change the system.

The pillars of apartheid include the official identification of all citizens by race; the restriction of the franchise to whites in parliamentary elections;

## Racial Distribution of South African Population 1980

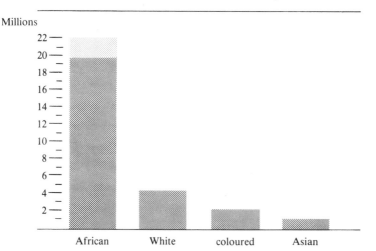

Figures are taken from *South Africa: Time Running Out,** which says: "Based on official reports which are generally believed to underestimate the number of Africans . . . . The 1980 figures are based on preliminary 1980 census results, plus estimates for the 'independent' homelands of the Transkei, Bophuthatswana, and Venda, which were not covered by the census. The figures omit Africans whose presence in 'white' areas is illegal under South African laws."

The graph indicates an estimate of twenty-two million Africans, probably a conservative figure for 1982. We have extended the first column to indicate this estimate.

---

*An excellent reference produced by a study commission on U.S. policy on South Africa, funded by the Rockefeller Foundation. See Appendix, p. 146.

restriction by race of areas for ownership and occupation of land and housing; control of black labor and mobility; a segregated, unequal education system; restricted personal and social interaction among groups. These are enforced by a range of wide-reaching security laws, applied by a sophisticated and powerful police and military force at the discretion of government leaders, the police themselves, or minor officials.

## Racial Identification

In South Africa racial identification determines all facets of a person's life. It determines minor aspects such as the bus stop at which to stand while waiting for the segregated bus; it determines major aspects such as the quality of education a person receives and the location of home and work; it determines economic, social and political rights.

The Population Registration Act of 1950 ensures that every person is assigned to a racial category—white, coloured or African. Since Asians (mostly Indians) were considered undesirable foreigners, they were not categorized separately. In practice, however, there are separate administrative departments for Asians in relation to education, residential and commercial areas and wages. Africans are further divided by ethnic group. Coloured people are those of mixed racial background, many tracing their heritage to the 17th century when the Dutch settled in the Cape Province.

The South African government has established boards which determine classification and may change it. The process of reclassification is usually traumatic and humiliating, since the basis for change includes family history and physical characteristics, such as the width of the nose or the type of hair. It has resulted in the separation of husband from wife, of parents from children, or sisters from brothers, since people of different races must live, learn, work and travel separately. In 1980, 152 persons had their race classification changed by South African officials.

## Restricted Franchise

In South Africa only whites, sixteen per cent of the population, may stand as candidates and vote in general elections and thus have a place or voice in the choice of Parliament. Blacks may vote for leaders in the townships and homelands and for members of ethnic councils. They have little enthusiasm for these political institutions, designed and assigned to them by whites. The institutions are perceived as having little power or influence. Since there is little constitutional limit on Parliament's authority, it retains the final legislative power in South Africa.

The limitation of the franchise to whites has developed during this century. Until 1936 some Africans in the Cape Province could vote, although only for whites. In 1956 coloureds were removed from the common elec-

*Two of Petra's teachers had asked to be present and volunteered their assurances that Petra Albertyn was one of the finest—Dr. Sterk cut them off: "We're not testifying to her quality. We're interested only in her race." And the way in which he spoke these words conveyed the clear impression that he now considered the accusations against this child justified. This encouraged the vice-principal to say that he had been watching Petra for some time, and she not only looked suspiciously dark, but she also behaved in distinctly Coloured ways.*

*"What do you mean?" Dr. Sterk asked.*

*"The way she says certain words."*

*Venloo's dominee, Reverend Classens, was a committee member and he asked ponderously, "Do we appreciate what we're doing here tonight? This child's entire future is at stake." "No one could be more sympathetic than we are, Dominee," Dr. Sterk said. "But if she is Coloured, then one of her parents must be Coloured, too. They can have a future among their own people. Not here in Venloo."*

*"Does this mean," the dominee asked, "that you plan to examine every child who seems a bit dark?"*

*"They are examined every day. By their fellow students. By everyone who sees them. This is a Christian nation, Dominee, and we obey the law."*

*"That is what I preach. But I also preach 'Suffer the little children to . . .'"*

*"We don't persecute little children. But we must keep serious priorities in mind."*

*"Such as?"*

*"The moral welfare of every child in this school."*

*After the meeting a grim-faced Dr. Sterk went to see the val Valcks, and reported: "I've seen the Albertyns and there is foundation for your accusations. The vice-principal has also had suspicions."*

*"That's what we told you," Mrs. van Valck said smugly. "What are you going to do about it?"*

*"I've asked the Albertyns to remove their daughter."*

*"And they refused?"*

*"They have." There was a long pause, in which each of the three considered the inevitable next step, the one that would throw the Community into turmoil. Twice Dr. Sterk made as if to speak, then thought better of it. In a matter of such gravity the decision must be made by people involved, and he would wait upon them.*

*Finally Leopold van Valck asked in a low voice, "You want to know whether we're prepared to lodge formal charges?"*

*"We are," his wife interrupted with great force. Having made the decision for all of them, she sat primly in her chair, hands folded, chin jutting out as if she were already bringing her testimony before the Race Classification Board.*

James A. Michener, *The Covenant*,
New York: Random House, 1980, p. 748.

toral roll in Cape Province and voting became a "whites only" privilege.

Not only is the vast majority of the population unable to vote; it is prohibited from indirect participation in national politics. There is not even a means for expression of opinion, much less political self-determination. In 1968 the Prohibition of Political Interference Act made it illegal for political parties to have interracial membership. Until that time, although blacks could not vote they could participate in the development of party policy and the selection of party leaders. The apartheid system has increasingly closed off avenues for meaningful political participation by Africans, and has attempted to divert their political energies into separate political entities.

In 1980 a reform was implemented upon recommendation of the Schlebusch Commission, to give Indian and coloured people an advisory capacity in government in the President's Council. This sixty-member body advises the President or Parliament, if either makes such a request. The members, chosen from whites as well as coloured and Asians, are appointed by the President. The reform seems of little significance, given its advisory and appointed nature. A number of coloured and Indian leaders refused to participate, and many of those who did participate became dissatisfied. Far more important, however, is the obvious fact that Africans, seventy percent of the population, are totally left out.

The Council has proposed that Asians and coloureds have some measure of representation in the all-white South African Parliament. The idea for this proposal was endorsed by Prime Minister Botha in February 1982. "Although the proposal seems to offer these groups greater participation than previous schemes, which have been overwhelmingly rejected among Asians and coloured, there were no signs that it would meet with any greater approval within the two communities" (*Africa News,* March 1, 1982). The immediate effect of Botha's endorsement of the idea in advance of the formal proposal was a right-wing split from the National Party.

## Land

Historically and systematically, apartheid began long before its proclamation in 1948. Its roots are embedded in the issue of land. British settlers and Afrikaners, the whites of Dutch and Huguenot background, realized that land was the key to any scheme of development in South Africa. This realization prompted the expropriation of African land, early by conquest, later by law. The 1913 Native Lands Act denied the right of Africans to buy white land and vice-versa. This, in effect made a *de facto* division: 87% of the land for whites, 13% for Africans. The Native Trust and Land Act of 1936 attempted to restrict Africa to the reserves, although millions of Africans continued to live in urban areas and on white farms as agricultural workers in compliance with influx control provisions or illegally.

These laws preceded the 1950 Group Areas Act which proclaimed strict residential segregation and became a cornerstone in apartheid's legal and economic structure. The Group Areas Act declared that South Africa was composed of African, coloured, Asian and white areas, and that each group had exclusive ownership and occupation rights within those areas. The 87/13 ratio was maintained; occupation was defined from the most temporary kind (such as "occupying" a movie theatre) to living an area. As such, the Group Areas Act is the foundation for the strict segregation of South African society. No black may own property in a white area; no black may occupy such land without special permission. The African areas were further divided according to ethnic differences among the African population.

Indians and coloureds were primarily affected by the Group Areas Act, as Africans had been restricted previously. Indians and coloured were allocated restricted areas within the white areas for their homes, shops, schools and hospitals (all segregated, of course). This entailed a massive uprooting and resettling process, which is not yet completed. Some whites were moved, but the comparative numbers speak eloquently of those who bore the heavier burdens. By the end of 1979 just over 2,000 white families had been forced to move, in comparison with 35,000 Indian and 75,000 coloured families. A well-known resettlement case is that of District Six of Cape Town. The district had been occupied by coloureds since 1834. In 1966 it was proclaimed a white area and coloured families were ordered to move. At that time the estimated population of District Six was 60,000 coloured, 800 whites.

Such numbers pale to insignificance when compared to those for African resettlement. A 1976 official government statement, quoted by a South African Council of Churches publication, said an estimated two million Africans had been resettled since 1948, and at least another million were to be moved to bantustans, or homelands. The bantustans are largely rural areas, designation by the South African government on the basis of ethnic group as "homelands" for Africans. The urban dweller who is resettled to a bantustan may have never seen it and have no ties there. But no consultation of choice is involved when a settlement order is given. The South African government insists that residential segregation is needed for racial peace. It has, in fact, brought much distress and tension in urban and rural areas.

Law and practice often differ in South Africa for practical or humanitarian reasons or just bureaucratic inefficiency. There are, for example, countless thousands of Africans living illegally in African urban areas, and coloured and Indians rent property in white areas. But at any moment the law may be enforced inhumanely and efficiently.

> *With every proclamation of a "separate" new tribal homeland,*
> *South Africa gives a cruel twist to the meaning of independence.*
> *Although their statehood is ushered in with ceremonies that ape*
> *decolonization—the lowering of South Africa's flag, the firing of*
> *a 101-gun salute—the policy is in fact a cynical effort to preserve*
> *white dominance in the richest regions and to strip South African*
> *blacks of their already limited citizenship.*
>
> *The New York Times,* editorial,
> December 12, 1981

The South African government proposes to make the ten homelands "in-dependent." The Transkei was the first homeland to be granted "in-dependence" by the South African government in 1976. It has been fol-lowed by Bophuthatswana in 1977, Venda in 1979 and Ciskei in 1981. No nation in the world but South Africa has yet recognized any of these homelands as independent states. Most of the homelands do not even con-sist of single geographic units (see map, p. 34). Bophuthatswana, for exam-ple, is made up of seven unconnected areas. There is little prospect that the homelands can be made economically viable. They receive 85% of their regular budget from the South African Parliament on an annual basis. A 1980 study by the South African Council of Churches refers to a develop-ment plan for Venda, prepared for the government by the African Institute in 1979. The minimum cost was estimated to be R94.7 million (94.7 million Rand) per annum from 1980 to 2000. (The Rand in early 1982 was worth $1.00.) South Africa would have to advance 80 to 90% of that. After five years of "independence" George Matanzima, Prime Minister of the Transkei said: "South Africa is not really interested in the development of Transkei. South Africa intended it to be a labor reservoir." (*New York Times,* 8/11/81) The South African Council of Churches reports:

> According to the Quail Report released on Feb. 20, 1980, Ciskei had 19% more people in the 0-14 and 65-plus age groups than South Africa at large; an unemployment rate of 39%; sub-sistence farming output of about R40 per head per year; and a resident gross national product of R180 per head per year, most of it derived from wage earnings in South Africa—where white per capita income averages R2,500 per year. "The most desired form of government (ninety per cent of all Xhosas polled) was a unitary state for the whole of South Africa on a one man, one vote basis. This was the most favoured solution right across the board on the part of urban and rural Ciskeians, old and young, male and female, poor and richer, traditional and detribalized."

The evolution of the bantustan to "independence" is an example of apar-theid's sophisticated nature. The South African government now has only nominal responsibility for the "independent" homeland, while in the past it was directly responsible both politically and economically for the bantustan.

These changes are all a part of the South African government's attempt to put a new face on apartheid. The ultimate goal of "separate development," as it is now called by the government, is the creation of African "independent" states. Africans would then have political rights and citizenship in their own "states," and would be left without even a claim to citizenship or political rights in South Africa itself. This situation is true already for those whom the government decrees are "citizens" of the "independent" homelands, whether they have ties there or live in a city hundreds of miles away. Citizenship is removed from South African residents by an act of the white Parliament or by administrative fiat.

> The four independent homelands have some 4.8 million resident and 3.3 million nonresident citizens, so it is factually correct to state that millions of fellow South Africans have been deprived of South African citizenship, an action that has angered and outraged many of them, many of their fellow-citizens, and the international community. (Dr. F.E. Auerbach, President, SAIRR,* *Race Relation News,* December 1981)

The homelands are reservoirs for the maintenance of cheap, controllable black labor. The population of the homelands is primarily the old, the sick, the very young, a disproportionate number of women, and men waiting to find work. Wage earners leave for work in the mines, the urban industrial areas or on white farms, sometimes hundreds of miles from their families. The wage levels are rarely enough to support the workers' families adequately, even with supplementary subsistence agriculture in the homelands. A South African newspaper, the *Sunday Tribune,* in 1976 quoted the results of a survey of the Nqutu district of KwaZulu, another homeland, but one which has refused "independence." It stated: "The average income of families of up to seven was R14.87 a month from migrant worker breadwinners. This would buy 2 bags of mealie meal** a month, at R7.20, leaving 47 cents over for other food and clothes."

The problem of survival is compounded by the high population density of the homelands. Inadequate wages and the attempt at what is less than subsistence agriculture in the homeland produce a life replete with health problems, nutritional deficiencies and high infant mortality. Inflation affecting basic costs such as food hits homeland Africans especially hard because of their limited resources.

---

*South African Institute of Race Relations, a voluntary organization in Johannesburg which does excellent work on race relations and collects factual information on South African racial problems.

**Ground white corn, the main item of traditional African diet.

> *Cholera, an infectious disease that thrives where there is an*
> *absence of clean drinking water and decent sanitation, has*
> *become endemic in South Africa's rural black "homelands" in*
> *the last two years . . . .*
> *Since the first cases were reported in the eastern Transvaal*
> *about 15 months ago, there have been nearly 7,000 confirmed*
> *cases of symptomatic cholera, resulting in at least 70 deaths. Only*
> *two whites, both laboratory technicians, and a small number of*
> *Indians in the province of Natal are known to have been infected.*
> *The rest have been blacks.*
> *Calculated on a per capita basis, South Africa now has a higher*
> *incidence of the disease than India and Indonesia, where it has*
> *long been endemic.*
>
> *The New York Times,* January 17, 1982

The South African Council of Churches passed a resolution at its 1979
conference. It detailed the reasons why "separate development," or the
movement toward "independent homelands" represents a human crisis in
South Africa:

   a)  dispossession of land when people are compulsorily removed
       and resettled in or near bantustans;

   b)  the government policy, illustrated in the Riekert report, of
       deepening the division between urban and rural people, and
       according privileges to a few at the expense of the many;

   c)  the policy of removing South African citizenship from all
       blacks;

   d)  economic and social policies which have reduced thousands
       of people to extreme poverty, hunger to the point of starva-
       tion, and hopelessness; and have destroyed the fabric of both
       family and community life for the larger part of South
       Africa's people.

It is not surprising in the face of the above, that the AFSC visitors to South
Africa in 1980 heard this overall policy described as genocide.


## Women and Apartheid

In every society women hold certain positions and perform certain functions different from those of men. Because women bear children, many of
their roles are often related to the support and nurturing of children and to
maintaining the households. When poverty is extreme, as in both the urban
townships and rural homelands of South Africa, the burden on women may
be especially heavy. A series of regulations, laws, customs and cultural expectations confine many women to the barest soil of the homelands where
they must attempt literally to scratch some life from the land. Because of
influx control and the limitations of rights, only one-fourth of African

women in South Africa are able to engage in paid employment; the others are confined to the homelands. These depend on the meager wages which can be earned in the cities and sent back to them by wage earning husbands to feed, clothe and house the children who are in their charge.

When women enter the paid labor force in South Africa, they experience additional hardships. As are men, they are separated from their children, even the newborns, as a condition for living and working in restricted white areas. They are paid less than men in virtually every occupation, and are confined to the lowest paid occupations. The 1970 census showed that ninety-one per cent of the female workforce was concentrated in service (domestic) and agricultural occupations. These are both low paid and subject to no regulation regarding minimum wage, work hours or benefits. Recognizing the particular susceptibility of domestic workers, the South African Institute of Race Relations recently undertook a project to organize domestic workers to standardize wages and to improve working conditions. This project also worked with white women employers as well as with black domestic workers.

In the liberation struggle, the challenge for women is twofold. While they seek freedom for their people, they also seek within that freedom their own equality with the men of their society. Women's organizations in community affairs have traditionally been strong in South Africa. In the 1940s women campaigned for food rations and attempted to organize food cooperatives when food prices were rising rapidly. In the early 1950s African women organized "cultural clubs" as alternative schools during school boycotts. Black women have also been active against resettlement and squatter removals. In 1978 at Crossroads and in 1980 at Phoenix township, near Durban, women led resistance against removal in ways which received international attention.

Nonetheless, women as workers and women as members of a society which regulates their activities and where they can live are the most vulnerable group in South Africa. In each aspect of apartheid the impact on women is particularly harsh. The effect on a society which distorts and abuses one-half of its adult population, which breaks up its families, and which impoverishes the caretakers of its children and the children themselves is incalculable.

## Control of Black Labor and Movement

The Stallard Commission in 1922 stated: "It should be a recognized principle of government that Natives—men, women and children—should be permitted within municipal areas insofar and for so long as their presence is demanded by the wants of the white population." This principle still seems to be in effect. Families are divided when men or women seek work in white areas unless they already have homes in the "location" attached to white cities and commute daily or weekly, according to the distance and their time off.

Until recently, no African could stay legally in a "prescribed area" (white area) for more than 72 hours unless he or she:

a)   was born in the area;

b   had worked for the same employer continuously for ten years or different employers for fifteen, and had lived in the area with no breaks;

c)   was the wife, unmarried daughter, or minor son of a qualified resident, as in a) or b);

d)   had permission from a labor bureau.

These qualifications are set out in the Black Urban Areas Consolidation Act of 1945, and are commonly named for the section of the act, Section 10 rights. There have been recent changes in this law resulting from recommendations of the Riekert Commission. Such changes affect only a small number of Africans. Urban Africans with established Section 10 rights may move to other townships, provided housing is available. This proviso amounts to a negation, since there are long waiting lists for housing in the townships. The changes make it increasingly difficult for newcomers to gain Section 10 rights.

Given such conditions, it follows that most African workers live apart from their families. Many live in single-sex hostels housing enormous numbers. Conditions were described in a South African newspaper, the *Rand Daily Mail* in June 1977: "The main barracks at Langa were built in 1927/28. They house 2,032 men with 24 men in each room . . . . In many cases the workers use cardboard to keep out the wind and for privacy. The sheds have no heating."

Contracts for such workers are now commonly awarded for 11 or 11½ months, at which time the worker must return to the bantustan to renew a contract and thus cannot develop Section 10 (b) residency qualifications. This was challenged in court in the Rikhoto case. Despite the annual brief returns to the homelands, the court agreed that "by any reasonable standards, employment was continuous" (*New York Times,* 11/1/81) and therefore Rikhoto was eligible for Section 10 (b) rights. The case is being appealed; regardless of that result, as the *New York Times* stated "the ultimate significance of the decision cannot be known until it becomes clear whether the government will let it stand," because Parliament can simply change the law if it wishes.

Few women qualify for Section 10 rights on their own. Thus women who have lived in an urban township for their entire lives as dependent daughters and wives are subject to removal if their husbands die, desert them or divorce them. Late in their lives and with no means of sustaining life, many women have found themselves removed to the homeland of their former husbands, where they have never been and where they have no family connections at all. Underlying the regulations regarding women's rights to live in urban areas is the belief that if women become permanent settlers in these areas, then South Africa runs the risk of an entrenched African population rooted there. To support the fiction of roots in the homelands the policy keeps women, as the centers of their families, based in the homelands to which men are then expected to return.

There are some cases where families remain together illegally. A highly publicized case was that of Crossroads, the squatter community outside Cape Town where women and children illegally joined the men who were working in the area. National and international pressure and demonstrations prevented the government from removing the squatters and destroying their shanties. But that case is exceptional. In August 1981, three thousand people, mostly women and children, were arrested at another location near Cape Town and, under a law which applies to non-South Africans, were sent back to Transkei where many face the possibility of malnutrition or even starvation. Employment for many Africans means the destruction of normal family life.

In the "prescribed areas," Africans live in townships or "locations," separated from the white cities where they work. These crowded areas are homes for both temporarily single workers and those families who qualify under Section 10 (a) and (b). Soweto, outside Johannesburg, is one of the best known of those townships. Government estimates place the population at 1.2 million, but unofficially figures of 1.5 to 2 million are given. Most houses are standardized with two, three or four rooms and built by the government. A four-room house may be occupied by an extended family of fifteen or sixteen persons. One-half hour from the glittering skyscrapers and swimming pools of Johannesburg lies the township of Soweto, which in 1979 was the subject of a survey cited by the authors of *South Africa: Time Running Out*. This survey indicated there were inside baths in 5.8% of the houses, inside toilets in 12.8%, running water (cold) in 21%. A white social worker who is well acquainted with Soweto regarded these figures with skepticism and urged they be considered as optimistic maximums. Streets are generally unpaved. In winter the red dust and acrid coal smoke sting the eyes and irritate the lungs. In windy weather there is also dust from the closely adjacent mine dumps. Recent improvements, such as electrification, are welcomed but do not remedy major grievances. Violence, born of overcrowding and frustration, is common.

Cases during the period, July 1, 1978 to June 30, 1979

| SOWETO | NO. OF CASES REPORTED |
|---|---|
| Murder | 648 |
| Rape | 1,151 |
| Culpable homicide | 230 |
| Assault with intent to do grievous bodily harm | 7,532 |
| Robbery | 3,549 |

Comparison of reported cases of crime by race for all of South Africa, 7/1/78–6/30/79

| CRIME | White/ white | White/ African | African/ white | African/ African |
|---|---|---|---|---|
| Murder | 125 | 83 | 93 | 6,207 |
| Rape & Attempted Rape | 423 | 249 | 199 | 14,245 |
| Assault | 1,783 | 942 | 1,375 | 121,563 |
| Culpable homicide (not motor accidents) | 79 | 17 | 129 | 3,414 |

*Survey of Race Relations in South Africa,* 1980,
South African Institute of Race Relations, p. 220.

These are conditions most whites do not see. Whites may not enter African townships except by specially issued permits and may be arrested, fined or imprisoned if found doing so.

Movement of Africans is closely controlled by the South African government. Labor bureaus, set up in the homelands by the Native Laws Amendment Act of 1952, and the mine recruitment offices dictate who may go where. They are the basic tools of effective regulation or migrant and contract labor. Jobs are offered through those offices; work-seekers register there and must receive permission to leave the homeland, even to look for work. This results in a tightly regulated supply of labor. Those who have secured jobs are confronted by the reserves of unemployed in the homelands. If they do not "behave," they can be "endorsed out," that is, sent back to the homelands; others, presumably more amenable to working conditions, will be recruited to replace them. White trade unions strongly reinforce these policies. White farmers also welcome a system that supplies them with cheap, compliant labor.

Low wages for Africans have been in the interest of employers and white unions. African wages in nonagricultural sectors are improving, as the need for skilled labor increases. From 1975 to 1979 the ratio of average white wages to average wages of Africans has dropped from 4.9:1 to 4.2:1. However, the following figures produced by the Afrikaanse Handels-instituut in 1980 show that the actual gap between African and white wages is increasing:

## AVERAGE EARNINGS — 1975-1979 IN SOUTH AFRICAN
## NON-AGRICULTURAL SECTOR

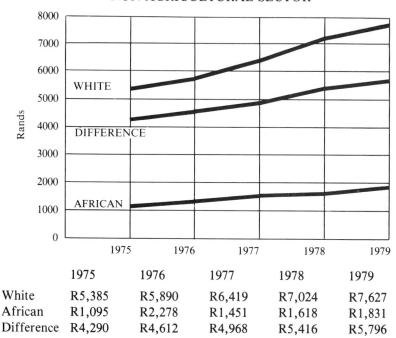

|            | 1975    | 1976    | 1977    | 1978    | 1979    |
|------------|---------|---------|---------|---------|---------|
| White      | R5,385  | R5,890  | R6,419  | R7,024  | R7,627  |
| African    | R1,095  | R2,278  | R1,451  | R1,618  | R1,831  |
| Difference | R4,290  | R4,612  | R4,968  | R5,416  | R5,796  |

(SAIRR, *Annual Survey,* 1980)

The "pass" which all Africans must carry is a key to the system known as influx control. The control of black labor, like the expropriation of land, began long before apartheid was a formal system. In 1809 a pass law was introduced in the Cape Province. It defined Khoikhoi men, one of the indigenous groups at the time of the Dutch arrival, who were not working for whites as vagrants and subject to punishment. Those who worked carried passes. Any white could demand to see the pass at any time. Ironically, the law establishing the present form of the pass is entitled Blacks Abolition of Passes and Coordination of Documents Act of 1952. Instead of abolishing passes, the act changed the name of the "pass" to "reference book" and required for the first time that women carry them as well as men. The reference book serves as an identification card and includes all employment information. Its various stamps indicate where an African may legally exist.

Failure to carry the reference book or have it in proper order results in arrest. AFSC visitors to South Africa in 1980 saw proceedings in a pass law court in which penalties of R50 or 90 days in jail were dispensed in two-minute trials. A 1976 survey by two University of Cape Town lecturers reported by the *Rand Daily Mail* indicated that half the African workers in the Cape Town area earned less than R25 a week. Therefore, a fine of R50 is substantial for those people. The South African Institute of Race Relations reported that in 1980 there were more than 300,000 arrests (almost 1,000 a day) "under laws restricting the movement of Africans." The system permits extensive harassment of Africans by police and magistrates. The plight of many people without the proper stamps in their pass is illustrated in the moving play, *Siswe Bansi is Dead.*

> *My passbook talks good English too, big words that Siswe can't read and don't understand. Siswe wants to stay here in New Brighton and find a job; passbook says, "No! Report back." Siswe wants to feed his wife and children; passbook says, "No. Endorsed out." They never told us it would be like that when they introduced it. They said: Book of Life! Your friend! You'll never get lost! They told us lies. ***

The need to control labor is a fundamental tenet of apartheid. African labor is the backbone of the strongest industrial complex on the African continent. As stated in *South Africa: Time Running Out:* "A web of statutes and regulations confines rural Africans to their tribal homelands and releases them only in the interests of white agriculture and industry" (p. 59).

## Education

Another key element in apartheid is the education system. Until 1953 education for Africans was offered by the central government, provincial governments, the churches, and communities. This provided a considerable variety of approaches and quality. Many African leaders in the rest of southern Africa were educated in some of the institutions in South Africa.

In 1953 the Bantu Education Act was passed, centralizing responsibility for education. Hendrik Verwoerd, then Minister of Native Affairs and later Prime Minister, introduced the bill saying: "When I have control of native education I will reform it so that the natives will be taught from childhood to realize that equality with Europeans is not for them." And later: "What is the use of teaching a Bantu child mathematics when it cannot use it in practice? . . . Education must train and teach people in accordance with their opportunities in life."

The resulting education for Africans has been a major source of frustration. Until the 1980s education was both free and compulsory for whites, but neither for Africans. African schools have been overcrowded and understaffed, and the curriculum has reflected Verwoerd's principles.

---

*Excerpt from *Siswe Bansi is Dead* by Athol Fugard, John Kani and Winston Ntshona. Copyright © 1973, 1974 by Athol Fugard, John Kani and Winston Ntshona. Reprinted by permission of Viking Penguin Inc.

According to the SAIRR *Race Relations News,* December, 1981, the teacher/pupil ratio for whites was 1:18 and for Africans was 1:48. Due largely to the 1976 Soweto uprising (see Chapter 4), which initially focused on the deficiencies of the education system, the Bantu Education Act was replaced in 1979 by the Education and Training Act, No. 90. The Act provides for the gradual introduction of compulsory education, free tuition and free schoolbooks for Africans. While the amount spent on African education has been rising steadily, there has not been the massive increase in the national education budget necessary for implementation of the Act. The priorities were made clear by Minister of National Education Punt Janson, in 1980. Defending the superiority of white education, he said: "We want to give white education the very best, and then we want to give the other people the best possible in the shortest possible time."

The Education and Training Act also provides that children will be educated in their ethnic language for the first four years. While this might appear educationally sound, it does not take into account the situation in South Africa. To teach in an ethnic vernacular, of which there are eight to ten in South Africa, when many children attend school for only four years, is to promote separation among Africans and to prevent many from learning a language that is more broadly used.

The Act does address the issue of whether subjects will be taught later in English or Afrikaans, a question with intense emotional impact. Parents will be able to have a say in that choice.

Nevertheless, these reforms do not touch the basic issue of the quality of education for Africans. AFSC visitors found one African family after another deeply concerned about the devastating and stunting effect of the education system. Many sacrifice time and money to find ways around the system. They turn to voluntary organizations to help fill the gap and meet needs through night schools, short courses and technical training. Private schools meet the needs of a few. According to a South African newspaper, the *Financial Mail,* 559 African pupils were attending 55 private schools in the Cape Province in 1980.

Major school boycotts and protests by coloured and African pupils in 1980 and 1981 indicate that change in education remains a primary issue. Both groups want a unified national education system. Posters in one of the 1980 demonstrations read: "Down With Tribal Education, Divide and Rule" and "South African Education Stultifies, Denies the Right of All to Grow Fully, Think Freely and Develop Our Potential." In the 1980 annual conference of Headmasters and Headmistresses of Private Schools of South Africa, the group agreed to send a telegram to Mr. Janson urging "the establishment, after consultation between all affected parties, of a unified, nonracial system of education which protects the individual rights of all South Africans." Pressure for change is being exerted by children, parents and educators. The De Lange Commission report of the Human Sciences

Research Council, submitted in late 1981, recommends further reforms. Yet there seems to be little change in the basic system which prompted a U.S. Congressional Study Tour (July 3–11, 1980) to report: "The South African government has used education as a political instrument to keep black South Africans in a semipermanent state of ignorance and economic deprivation."

## Restricted Social Interaction

The social lives of all South Africans are restricted by the apartheid system. The Prohibition of Mixed Marriages Act of 1949 and the Immorality Act of 1950 and 1957 seek to control the most intimate of relationships. While there has been some relaxation in the segregation of sports due to international boycotts, laws such as the Group Areas Act inhibit integrated sports. The relaxation takes place through the use of permits or by non-enforcement of laws rather than by a change in the law, which would indicate a yielding on principle.

---

*We can never remind ourselves too frequently just how blasphemous a creed apartheid really is. It seeks to do nothing less than obliterate the image of God in a large part of humanity. Firstly, it denies black people the right to be. It forces them to conform to an image which the Master Race has created of them . . . . This philosophy of black inferiority is enshrined in South Africa's laws and customs and prevents the black people from being themselves—themselves not as whites see them but as God has made them. . . .*

*Secondly, apartheid denies it victims the right to belong. Through its policy of racial segregation, it imposes unnatural divisions on society, choosing a quite irrelevant standard, that of skin pigmentation, to fix the boundaries of community . . . . It is morally indefensible, economically mad and politically explosive . . . . .*

*Thirdly, apartheid denies its victims the right to have. The Charter of the United Nations Organization lays down certain fundamental human rights which all persons possess for no other reason than the fact they are human . . . . Every man, woman and child has a right to a place at the feast of life and the main policy drive of any enlightened nation must be to reduce those inequalities which rob human beings of their chances through no fault of their own.*

Kenneth Kaunda, *The Riddle of Violence*
San Francisco: Harper & Row, 1980, pp. 174–77.

Hotels and restaurants may apply for permits to serve blacks as well as whites. But the basic law segregating public facilities, the Reservation of Separate Amenities Act of 1953, remains on the books. In fact few South African blacks or whites meet except in a master–servant or employer–employee relationship. Social interactions are severely restrained by law and custom. The rich potential of a variety of human relationships in South Africa remains untapped.

## Enforcement and Security Laws

The South African government has enacted a series of laws to enforce the apartheid system and to prevent change. The most basic laws are the Suppression of Communism Act of 1950, the Terrorism Act of 1967 and the Internal Security Act of 1976. These laws support the state in almost any action to neutralize or destroy opposition. "Communism" and "terrorism" are defined broadly by the South African government. In the Internal Security Act, the definition of communism includes any doctrine which "aims at bringing about any political, industrial, social or economic change within the Republic by the promotion of disturbance or disorder, by unlawful acts or omissions" or which "aims at the enrouragement of hostility between the European and non-European races of the Republic" where the consequences are calculated to further the kind of changes defined above. Peaceful but effective resistance campaigns are thus defined as "communist." The Terrorism Act is even broader, and includes as terrorist acts "to cause substantial financial loss to any person or to the State," or "to embarrass the administration or the affairs of State."

Detention without charge is a major tool used by the South African government to suppress dissent. From 1963 to 1967 detention became legal for 90, then 180 days, and finally for an indefinite period. At this time, a person merely *suspected* of terrorism, as defined above, may be held without charge or trial for an indefinite period of time, at the sole discretion of a police officer the rank of Lieutenant Colonel or above. The courts are expressly prohibited from intervening. In 1976 a law was passed authorizing the Minister of Justice to detain any person he suspects of being a danger to the state security or public order, even without dependence on the broad Terrorism Act.

In all cases, detention may include solitary confinement and torture. Winnie Mandela, wife of Nelson Mandela, the imprisoned leader of the African National Congress, was held in solitary confinement in the late 1970s for seventeen months. She was never charged with a crime. She continues to be confined to a limited rural area and was served in January 1982 with her fifth five-year banning order.

Banning is another method used to silence critics of South African government policies and the apartheid system. The Internal Security Act authorizes banning, a totally arbitrary procedure, with no recourse or appeal. No reasons need be given. Most banning orders restrict a person for five years and can be renewed. They prohibit the person from speaking publicly, being quoted, and entering educational institutions, publishing houses or courts. The orders commonly restrict the number of people a banned person may see at one time, usually to one. A banned person is usually not allowed to leave a magisterial district. Normal employment or social life is generally impossible. Banning orders are served primarily against blacks, but whites are also included. The extensive bannings of October 19, 1977 included that of Donald Woods, a white newspaper editor, and Beyers Naude, a white Dutch Reformed minister and founder of the Christian Institute, which challenged apartheid.

The threat of detention and banning, both arbitrary and unchallengeable procedures, resulting in anything from social isolation to death is an effective means of intimidating those who would critize or change the apartheid system. There have been a number of deaths among political prisoners in detention. The most recent was that of Dr. Neil Aggett, a white union leader who was reported to have hanged himself February 5, 1982. He is the first white to die in detention. Among blacks, the death of Black Consciousness leader, Steve Biko, is one of the better known. He was detained on the 18th of August, 1977 in good health. Twenty-six days later he was dead. These grim facts are not disputed by the South African government:

1. Biko was held naked in solitary confinement from the 19th of August to the 6th of September.

2. He was taken to the interrogation room on the 6th of September. That night he was handcuffed and shackled by leg irons locked to the walls and left to sleep that way.

3. He was not removed from the irons for two days, by which time he was mentally confused; his hands, feet and ankles were swollen and cut; his clothes and blankets were soaked in urine.

4. He was taken naked in the back of a landrover 750 miles to a prison hospital. He was given a mat and died on the stone floor of his cell.

The chief magistrate of Pretoria absolved the security police of any responsibility, and the South African government has never admitted any irregularity in Biko's treatment. Biko was the twenty-fourth person to die between March 19, 1976 and September 12, 1977 while being held in detention without charge in South Africa.

"Fifty-two persons died in detention between 1963 and 1978, according to U.S. State Department's latest annual report on human rights abuses, but police always have claimed death was due either to suicide or accident" *(The Washington Post,* February 19, 1982). Those in opposition to the regime are often frightened with threats, wearied, harassed and even killed. The system seeks to break them by the security apparatus and a fearsome petty bureaucracy.

The security system is enforced by the police (nationalized), by the special Department of National Security and by the military. There are, however, other means of controlling opposition to apartheid. There is considerable control of the press. While criticism of the government does appear in the press, there are actually quite extensive limitations to its freedom. "The appearance of a healthy press and liberty of expression is false." said Anthony Matthews, a Professor of Law at the Unversity of Natal in Durban. Pressure is maintained on the national press association to police their members regarding stories with "negative racial overtones." The Defense Act of 1957 and the Official Secrets Act prevent publication of any unauthorized information about the South African military. Because of these laws news of the South African army invasion of Angola in 1975 was not published in South Africa until long after the world knew about it. The Police Act of 1958, amended in 1979, makes it illegal to publish articles criticizing police behavior. The Prisons Act of 1959 forbids criticism of prisons. Newspapers can be closed and lose their R20,000 registration deposit, as has happed to African papers, *The World* in 1977, and the *Post* and *Sunday Post* in January 1981. Donald Woods, exiled South African journalist, explained in his autobiography: "The Government had at its disposal more than twenty statutes governing what could be published in newspapers, and several of these laws empowered them to close down any newspaper arbitrarily, without court proceedings, and to jail or ban any editor without explanation" (Asking for Trouble [New York: Atheneum, 1981] p. 9).

The Steyn Commission of Inquiry into the Media made recommendations in early 1982 for further restrictions and control. These include the licensing of journalists and the setting up of a government controlled council to monitor and discipline journalists.

The government can also outlaw organizations under the Unlawful Organizations Act of 1960. Eighteen organizations were so banned in October 1977, losing their property to the State. Under the Riotous Assemblies Act of 1956, amended in 1974, the government can forbid meetings and gatherings, either private or public, with two or more people.

The South African government uses a wide variety of tools to prevent changes in the apartheid system. They range from intimidation, to control of information, to overt violence. The laws permit wide use of unchallengeable discretionary power, leaving the opponent of apartheid under constant threat, and keeping government officials increasingly out of touch with the level of anger and bitterness of its people, as well as with the strength of demand for change.

In the face of the pervasive system of apartheid, its denial of human values, its ruthless enforcement system, the human spirit remains indomitable. This untitled poem is by Dennis Brutus, an exiled black South African:

> Somehow we survive
> and tenderness, frustrated, does not wither.
>
> Investigating searchlights rake
> our naked unprotected contours;
>
> over our heads the monolithic decalogue
> of fascist prohibition glowers
> and teeters for a catastrophic fall;
>
> boots club the peeling door.
>
> But somehow we survive
> severance, deprivation, loss.
>
> Patrols uncoil along the asphalt dark
> hissing their menance to our lives,
>
> most cruel, all our land is scarred with terror,
> rendered unlovely and unloveable;
> sundered are we and all our passionate surrender
>
> but somehow tenderness survives.*

## Whites and Apartheid

The South African government has been controlled by the National Party since 1948. This party is dominated by Afrikaners, who formally and deliberately brought apartheid into being. But its roots go back to the Act of the Union in 1910 and earlier, and will be more fully discussed in the next chapter. Here we note that the foundation of apartheid can be found in the culture and religion of the Afrikaners, as well as in its pragmatic acceptance by the English-speaking part of South Africa's white population.

The Afrikaans word apartheid is pronounced *a-par-tate* and means "apartness." This is seen as a means of maintaining cultural identity for the Afrikaners and others. In this theory, separation is the natural way of life because it allows groups to develop in their own way, with their own customs and languages. Hence the term "separate development" is now

---

*A Simple Lust* (New York: Farrar, Straus and Giroux, 1973), p. 4.

used officially instead of apartheid. It is clear, however, that the promotion and protection of Afrikaner culture is predicted on white control of land and resources, of politics and economics. Whites must dictate where and how others will develop. Afrikaners seem to believe that their cultural survival is synonymous with their domination and control of South Africa.

The religion of the Afrikaners is Dutch Reformed, a Calvinistic form of Protestantism, which will be discussed more fully in the next chapter. We only note here that religion contributed to a sense that Afrikaners were a "chosen people," with both mandate and responsibility to dominate and control South Africa.

Cultural preservation and religion are mixed in the Broederbond, a society of "brothers" formed in 1918 to promote the interests of the Afrikaners. In 1928 it became a secret society. Varioius exposes of the society indicate that its membership is exclusively white, male, Calvinist and Afrikaner. Since the National Party has been in power, there has been a remarkable overlap between the Broederbond and the highest officials in government, in the Dutch Reformed Church, in education, in the media, and in the civil service and transportation system. The "brothers" have served as the ideological architects of the South African State of today and as the chief promoters and defenders of apartheid. Debate on policy is reported to take place both in the Cabinet and the Broederbond Executive Committee. The fact that most the Cabinet members are "brothers" makes it difficult to delineate their roles clearly. Thus, the government is deeply influenced by a secret society, committed first and foremost to the Afrikaner people and their interests. While there have been disagreements within the Broederbond, a high priority is placed on a united front in defense of the State. The secret society stifles any moves toward inclusion of the vast majority of South Africa's population in the decision making.

Apartheid as a coherent theory was conceived by Afrikaners. Yet some of its key policies or directions were developed while the English-speaking whites were in control of South Africa, up to 1948. Apartheid is still supported by the English-speaking population. They have shown little initiative or leadership in the political arena to challenge the National Party. Until recently they held a monopoly on the economic power in South Africa, a power based on their control of rich natural resources and on cheap labor. Many thus actively participate in the exploitation of South Africa's black population and resources. Others insulate themselves from the horrors of apartheid and support the paternalistic view of Afrikaners that whites know best, will care for blacks, and therefore deserve to stay in control. All who benefit from apartheid become its accomplices, despite verbal protests to the contrary.

It is true that most white liberals emerge from the English-speaking population. But many Africans question how far such liberals will go in supporting fundamental change. In 1980, for example, white liberal students supported the school and university boycotts. But when threatened with explusion and denial of their degrees, they returned to classes. Not so the Africans and coloureds, who faced similar penalties. In this case and others, while some speak in opposition to apartheid, few seem ready to give up their privilege as part of the necessary transformation of their society. The contribution of whites who resist and criticize apartheid should not be ignored, but it must be acknowledged that the system is supported by the vast majority of English-speaking whites as well as by Afrikaners, through active participation in design as with the Broederbond, or in implementation, perhaps because of economic benefit, apathy or the fear of losing control and an unknown future.

Apartheid, as a deliberate public policy, has given race a class definition. Whites are South Africa's upper class, and blacks are the lower class. Apartheid has assigned to the white portion of South Africa's population, on the basis of its physical characteristics, control of all the political mechanisms of the state, the dispensation of the gains of the majority's labor, and the ultimate power to chart and direct the cultural and social interaction of the entire nation. It is a system of rigidities, resisting the organic growth and constructive mutations found in most societies. In fact, it tightens and entrenches itself under the growing miasma of fear. Any adaptations are improvised to protect the white power structure and do not alter apartheid fundamentally.

Those opposed to apartheid tend to see it in terms of its tragic impact on blacks, for it is blacks who bear most of the oppression. For whites also, however, apartheid has serious negative effects. There are whites, both Afrikaners and English-speaking, whose opposition to apartheid has caused them to be banned, imprisoned, harassed by their fellow citizens, and killed. Some of these have felt it necessary to go into exile.

Such impact on whites is easy to see, but apartheid has negative effects even on those who support it. There are dehumanizing consequences of the oppression of people and a psychological price for racial arrogance and separation. There is a deprivation from lack of friendship on the basis on equality with persons or rich cultural diversity.

White South Africans of all shades of political opinion carry feelings of guilt, fear and defensiveness which become evident in the most casual conversation with visitors when apartheid is mentioned. Apartheid is a burden for *all* South Africans. And the resulting violence, explicit and acute or implicit and chronic, damages all.

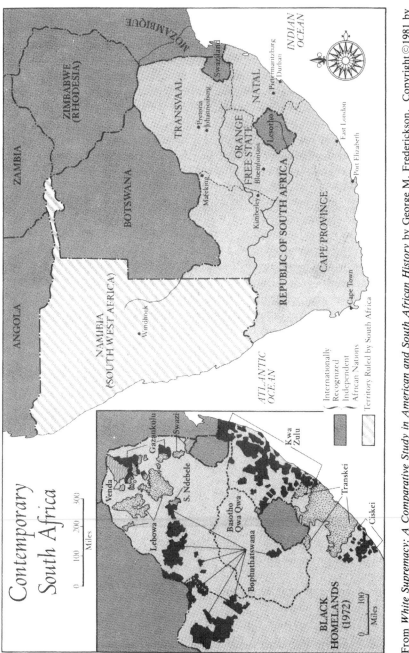

## Contemporary South Africa

From *White Supremacy: A Comparative Study in American and South African History* by George M. Frederickson. Copyright ©1981 by Oxford University Press, Inc. Reproduced by permission.

# CHAPTER 3

# *South African Background*

Apartheid in South Africa today can best be understood through a brief review of the historic forces that have molded the present society. The recent story is one of conflicts among peoples with different ideologies, group interests, and national designs, all rooted in the past.

The history of South Africa properly begins with the emergence of humanity on the continent. But we are concerned here with the recent era that gave rise to the problems—political, economic and human—which our paper addresses. Whether one regards this story as depicting the conquest of a subcontinent and its economic development by European settlers or the struggle for survival by Africans as dignified, self-defining people against the encroachments of foreign invaders, the constant theme of conflict between European and the indigenous people has persisted from the mid-seventeenth century to the present. How did it develop? When did the rivalry for territory become explicit racial exploitation? We will summarize, with a Eurocentric focus, the interactions that led to today's situation.*

The arrival of the Europeans to stay began at the Dutch provisioning station in the Cape of Good Hope in 1652. The area was then populated by nomadic people, the Khoikhoi (often called Hottentots) and the San (often called Bushmen). Their eastern neighbors were the migratory Bantu-speaking people, notably the Xhosa, Zulu, Tswana, Sotho and many smaller ethnic groups. Despite official statements about "an empty subcontinent," evidence suggests that representatives of these black groups were already occupying large portions of the greater Cape area. The Dutch soon expanded beyond the original station for the Dutch East India Company and gradually developed a settlement area for Europeans wishing to start fresh in another temperate part of the world. Over time, the Company controlled, curbed or displaced the indigenous people to provide for arriving European settlers. There was resistance to this presence almost immediately (see Chapter 4).

The early colonists were much influenced by their religious origins. Most of the Dutch were committed Calvinists, adhering to the theology of the Reformed Church. Their numbers were later augmented by the arrival of

---

*See Chronology, p. 133.

Huguenots who were fleeing their French homeland after the revocation of the Edict of Nantes in 1685, which for a century had permitted religious pluralism in that otherwise Catholic land. The Huguenots merged into the Dutch population and, as Calvinists, became members of the Dutch Reformed Church. Both groups left Europe prior to the French Revolution and in their isolation rarely felt the influence of liberalizing ideas that originated there.

As the numbers of Europeans increased, the competition for land and cattle with the much more populous indigenous Africans grew more intense. By the eighteenth century, the San, to escape annihilation, had retreated into the Kalahari desert. The cattle-herding Khoikhoi were more willing to accommodate, but no successful *modus vivendi* in the economic competition could be achieved. They were pushed into the interior and decimated by ruthlessness and disease. During a century of close interaction at the southern tip of the continent, the mixing of the races produced the "Cape Coloured" population. But to the east the larger number of Africans were much more inclined to resist European incursions into what they felt was their territory. Thus "Frontier Wars" marred the late eighteenth century, much as "Indian Wars" long occupied North Americans. The frontier line moved slowly eastward, and later northward as white military might drove African farmers and herders back.

Typical European use of grazing areas (staking out of portions for individual use) brought them into frequent conflict with the more nomadic Africans who used the grasslands for their herds in the traditional communal-ownership manner. The clashes between the two groups resulted in the Dutch (now Afrikaners*) accumulating more cattle and subjugating Khoikhoi as servants or slaves. Afrikaner nationalists look back to the late eighteenth and early nineteenth centuries as the beginning of a clearly defined emergence of European communities tied to the African land. While holding to a strong identification with their European heritage, they relinquished their ties to a specific homeland, and established a pattern of intense independence.

A common identification as Christians helped to unify the Europeans against the numerous African ethnic groups of the area. Indigenous people felt the increasing pressures of European encroachment, both physical and psychological. Missionaries brought a new religion that raised fundamental challenges to their traditions and tended to divide them. Many indigenous people accepted Christianity, some adapting it to their religious customs

---

*At that time, the Dutch were known as Boers (farmers). For convenience we will generally use the present-day term, "Afrikaner."

while others held to their traditional beliefs. Other Christian denominations were represented among later European immigrants. The importation of Asian laborers in the nineteenth century brought Hindu and Muslim faiths from India, adding to the rich religious mosaic, and to divisions among racial groups.

## Advent of the British

At the turn of the nineteenth century, international politics intervened in South Africa. As part of the Napoleonic Wars, the British first occupied The Cape Province in 1795, then permanently in 1806; the territory was ceded to the British by Holland in 1814. In 1820 the British began to send in numbers of colonists, many ex-soldiers, who established settlements along the coast to the east of Cape Town. British colonial political control made the Dutch settlers restive, due partly to the emergence of nineteenth century British liberalism. Impositions included making English the offical language in 1828, and the abolition of slavery throughout the British Empire in the 1830s. These two events weighed heavily with the Dutch in South Africa as infringements on their economic and cultural activities. On the economic side, the Dutch had already begun a rather extensive exploitation of the indigenous population and had imported slaves from the Far East and East Africa. On the cultural side, they feared they would lose their language and cultural identity. In great resentment, many Dutch settlers moved eastward and northward in an attempt to escape British hegemony. This great trek of 1936 became known as the "Voortrekker Movement."

The trek and the conflicts that it generated, coupled with Afrikaner psychological and religious needs, molded a people, a "Volk." The links that were forged created an Afrikaner legend which supported their belief in their right to conquer the lands and people that lay before them.

The Afrikaners wanted to achieve a utopian society as a "chosen people" dedicated to God. The Bible, especially the Old Testament, became their guide and defense. But their desire for isolation was soon thwarted. The discovery of diamonds in Kimberly in 1867, followed by that of gold in the Transvaal in 1884, attracted large numbers of chiefly English-speaking fortune hunters. The indigenous Africans, already exploited by the Afrikaners, now suffered under the encroachment of the British. To the Afrikaners, this influx of aliens seemed impious and coarse, threatening their way of life. But they could not stop the invasions. The "mineral revolution" that resulted transformed South Africa from an economically marginal area into an important participant in the world capitalist economy and an increasingly industrialized nation in its own right. The country was led in this direction by mining magnates, such as Cecil Rhodes, who became involved in the politics of the subcontinent, hoping to extend British imperial control northward.

The rivalry between the British and the Afrikaners culminated at the end of the nineteenth century in the second Anglo-Boer War (called the "Boer Wars" by the British, "Wars of Freedom" by the Afrikaners). In conventional warfare, armaments and manpower, the British always had the upper hand, but the Boer commandos, organized into effective guerrilla units, fought fervently for their homes and freedom. The British responded with a scorched earth policy, which brought great suffering and many deaths to the civilian population. Large numbers were put in internment camps. After fierce and prolonged fighting, the British prevailed. In 1902 they offered the Afrikaners a reconciling peace (which has been characterized by some persons as an attempt by the British to salve their consciences). Yet the bitterness of the conflict produced an enmity that has never been completely forgotten. Some of the generosity of the peace terms came at the expense of the Africans, for the terms reestablished absolute Afrikaner control over the local African population in the Orange Free State and the Transvaal. African leaders protesting this control were ignored. Also ignored were liberals and anti-imperialists in Britain, many of whom had opposed the war from its beginning, who generally supported the reconciling peace terms but were ineffectual in securing rights for Africans.

> *British Quakers and that staunch Anglican, Emily Hobhouse, with whom they worked closely, were among the war's opponents. Interestingly, South Africa's second submarine was recently named. "The Emily Hobhouse." Military leaders may have overlooked her equally fervent campaign to prevent and to end World War I, an effort inspired by Christian pacifism, not partisanship.*

### The Union

The Union of South Africa (now the Republic of South Africa) was created in 1910, with four provinces—two predominately British (Cape Province and Natal) and two Afrikaner (Orange Free State and Transvaal). The Union was more than a loose federation of relatively autonomous provinces, since the central government could control all areas. It was in fact operated by coalitions led by Afrikaner generals. Though the Union remained a British territory, English-speaking citizens tended to turn to business, mining and commerce, leaving Union politics by default to Afrikaner intellectual and religious leaders, such as General Jan Smuts, who worked through the United Party.

From the end of the Anglo–Boer War until 1948 when they finally gained control of the government, the most intensely nationalistic section of the Afrikaner population set as its goal the recovery of their traditional Volk unity and power through cultural and political efforts. Loosely bound together by their sense of grievance and cultural affinity, they formed a growing political strength, as their population expanded more rapidly than that of the English and as they could cooperate in political organization and maneuvering. The successful National Party, in power since 1948, was the result. Their leaders sought to free South Africa from the "yoke" of British imperial control; the first step of achieving dominion status in 1926 was confirmed in the statute of Westminister in 1931. The Declaration of the Republic in 1961 finally ended British political responsibility. A combination of factors brought this action. The referendum on the Republic was in fact passed by a tiny majority of white South Africans, a further evidence of the English-speaking South Africans' political weakness. The Afrikaners' longstanding desire for complete independence was heightened by their discontent at being drawn into a "British imperialist war" in 1939, and they were increasingly uncomfortable in a British Commonwealth of Nations which now included black nations. A change from Union to Republic required a review of membership. Prime Minister H. F. Verwoerd soon discovered in 1961 that black members of the Commonwealth would reject any reapplication, so none was made.

By the mid-twentieth century, Afrikaner leaders were beginning to diversify their economic base. While many remained attached to the land, an increasing number entered commerce and industry. Financial institutions appeared, catering to their constituency. The professions—law, teaching, investment counseling and others—attracted Afrikaner young people. This brought them into contact with English-speaking counterparts and the wider world of business and international finance. Some even began to see that the restrictions of the apartheid system were handicaps to their capitalistic ventures. For example, businesses were prevented from hiring black workers except for menial roles. This added to their labor costs when they had to pay artifically high wages to white workers. Few, however, abandoned their commitment to the National Party, where ideology overruled economics (as in the U.S. South in the early days).

The party was bolstered by Afrikaner economic strength, based on farmers, miners and the industrialized blue-collar workers. The better off members of the party tended to join the affluent urban dwellers who enjoyed the fruits of a thriving economy. This prosperity was based on abundant resources, the inflated value of gold, a patronizing government that usually protected white (Afrikaner) workers, diversification, and a seemingly limitless supply of cheap black labor. Their religious and cultural tradition interpreted their advantages as rewards for faithfulness to ordained rules and as their rightful destiny. Blinded or unaware of the suffering of the majority, aware of their own earlier hardships and disadvantages, and increasingly alarmed by the danger of losing their way of life, they voted for the continuance of the system.

South Africa today is in a dynamic but dangerous state of cross currents and tensions. Since their 1981 elections (and the U.S. elections shortly before) the government talks less of reforms or changes. Feeling threatened from the right within their party, and badgered by the more liberal and outspoken Parliamentary opposition, the cabinet appears to have become stymied. Meanwhile, frustration grows in many quarters at the apparent drift. The National Party is divided, though it might unite to preserve the status quo. White trade unions, always a political power, are worried by the growing influence of black unions. English-speaking South Africans and foreign nationals doing business are restive under the restrictive legislation, often based on race, that inhibits their capitalistic enterprise. Some venture into the uncharted land of experimental personnel reforms and benefits for their black employees. They are usually responding to pressures from Europe or America. Without such pressures they traditionally accepted the status quo as something to be lived with.

Government economists, worried about the country's prosperity in 1982, have helped produce important budget changes in the latest budgets that carry social implications. More funds are being allocated not only to defense, but also modestly into social and welfare programs that will benefit blacks. They will help erode petty apartheid further and provide wage and salary increases, designed to help counteract inflation for lower class workers. An Afrikaner economist was reported to have expostulated that these budgetary changes would bring the end of apartheid in the cause of national economic develpment. Of course, the unwanted unemployed are still being returned to the misery of the economic morass of "homelands."

Meanwhile the black community is becoming more organized and articulate in denouncing those aspects of apartheid that continue most to plague them. Patterns of leaderwhip are changing; while older names are still regarded, new ones appear, and some leadership never surfaces. Old issues and complaints remain, but are newly articulated and made relevant. Examples of changing tactics can be found in Soweto. The Urban Council and the Committee of Ten are finding new roles. "Homeland" leaders, such as Gatsha Buthelezi and his "cultural" organization, Inkatha, are receiving increased support from the black community. There seems to be more consultation among Africans, coloureds, and Indians. Banned liberation organizations, such as the African National Congress (ANC) and the Pan Africanist Congress (PAC) are stepping up covert and often violent activities. The government usually responds with harsher repressions. It is not easy to identify all the forces working in opposition to the apartheid system. This leaves government officials anxious and wary, making concessions here, tightening up there. Africans do not feel the balance tilting in their favor and press for more meaningful actions, using whatever means and organizations are available to them. The feeling of stagnation or retrogression builds up pressure for change.

Those who attempt to stay up to date and relevant are often frustrated by developments, some of them obvious, more of them obscure and not clearly analyzed. But the key question of power seems engraved in granite.

We now turn to topics that affect the current scene, but have roots deep in South African history.

## Namibia

Since World War I, South Africa has extended its power over neighboring Namibia (called South West Africa until recently). South West Africa was administered as a German colony from 1884 until 1915 when South African forces invaded. Germans had settled in the area, living along the coast and in the better watered lands of the north central plateau. Prior to World War I, African resistance led to a German order of extermination, in which 50,000–75,000 Herero and Nama people were killed and their land and cattle confiscated. The remaining people had little choice but to work for whites. After the end of World War I, the League of Nations gave to South Africa the administrative authority over South West Africa as a mandated territory. Article 22 of the Covenant of the League of Nations states, "The well-being and development of such peoples form a sacred trust of civilization." South Africa reported annually to the League of Nations Permanent Mandates Commission until the collapse of the League in 1939. During this time South Africa violently suppressed rebellions by different African groups—the Ovambo, who make up half of Namibia's black population, the Nama, and the Rehoboth people, called Basters. South Africa also imposed restrictive legislation on South West Africa, including regulations controlling movement of "natives" and the creation of "reserves" where "natives" were to live. These reserves were mostly on poor agricultural land in the south or in the sands of the Kalahari desert. From the beginning, the intent of South Africa seemed to be to absorb the territory.

After World War II the United Nations created a Trusteeship Council to take responsibility for the League's mandated territories. South Africa contested this action, and other former League members and the UN General Assembly sought an advisory opinion from the International Court of Justice. Both this ruling and another twenty-one years later came down against South African control. In 1971 the International Court reached the following conclusions about Namibia: "that the continued presence of South Africa in Namibia being illegal, South Africa was under an obligation to withdraw its administration immediately and thus put an end to its occupation of the Territory; that UN members and nonmembers were under obligation to recognize the illegality of South Africa's presence in Namibia and to refrain from acts which might imply recognition of the legality of South Africa's presence and administration.'' South Africa ignored this ruling, as it had the previous one.

From 1946 to 1966 the UN set up a number of committees and initiatives to deal with South Africa's role in South West Africa. In 1966 the General Assembly declared South Africa's mandate over South West Africa terminated, and placed the Territory under the direct responsibility of the UN. In the same year, the South West African People's Organization (SWAPO), organized in 1960 as a nationalist liberation movement, began its armed struggle for independence. In 1967 the General Assembly of the UN established the UN Council for South West Africa as the only legal authority to administer the Territory until independence, and appointed a UN Commissioner for South West Africa. In 1968 the territory was officially renamed Namibia by the UN (although South Africa does not recognize this name). Just as South Africa refused to accept the termination of the mandate, it has also ignored UN machinery to administer Namibia. Important recent developments on Namibia are reported in Chapter 6.

Thus, for most of this century, South Africa has controlled Namibia, in the face of increasing world disapproval. It has extended its apartheid rules and security legislation as well as its military power to Namibia, where the South African Defense Forces operate. While South Africa remains reluctant to grant independence, the people of Namibia seek world support. Before being sentenced to Robben Island, the Namibian leader Hermann Toivo ja Toivo said from the dock in 1966: "We feel that the world as a whole has a special responsibility toward us. This is because the land of our fathers was handed over to South Africa by a world body. It is a divided world, but it is a matter of hope for us that it at least agrees about one thing—that we are entitled to freedom and justice . . . .''

## The Dutch Reformed Church

The church has long been a prime factor in preserving and building Afrikaner culture. This culture comprises the new Afrikaans language, the Reformed religion, and other aspects of "tribal memory," reinforced by the record of recent persecution and earlier the experience of concentration camps established by the warring British forces, into which women and children were herded, 26,000 of whom died during the Anglo–Boer War of 1894–1902. Preachers from the pulpits and theologians imbued with this bitterness produced a negative doctrine. They built up the strength of the faith, the theology of separation, and belief in the purity of their race and their ethnic group within the white community.

The church's traditional isolation from European thought was scarcely modified. As contacts with the motherland were severed, Afrikaners, until

World War II, tended to be "platteland farmers." What the devout Afrikaners saw of the urban, predominately English-speaking communities repelled them. Their clergy insisted that they retain traditional rural values and their distinct culture, emphasizing strong family ties and their profound religious heritage. Not involved in urban commerce, they turned more to politics. Their political organizations, most of which had a strong religious bent, operated on the British parliamentary model. This trend culminated in 1948 in the capture of the Union government by a militant wing of the National Party. Their first Prime Minister, Dr. D.F. Malan, was a dominee or minister of the Dutch Reformed Church (DRC). Many of the cabinet members and most of the Prime Ministers were trained at the Afrikaans-language University of Stellenbosch. Their political platforms reflect strong religious and theological views.

The Dutch Reformed Church must not be seen as an "established church" like the Anglican Church of England, yet the alliance of government and church strengthened the commitment and outreach of both. Daughter missionary Dutch Reformed Churches grew among Africans, coloureds and Indians in the twentieth century, as did activities of outreach and service, not only in the Union but beyond to neighboring areas. But contrary to the experience of other churches, the Dutch Reformed Church was never in favor of an integration of congregations, theological schools, or synods. The black churches were intended to be completely separate, and their leadership was provided from the European or white clergy.

Eventually theological training schools were set up for the blacks. All of the instruction was in Afrikaans and led by Dutch Reformed white professors. Church leaders did not foresee that the black theologians would soon rise to prominence as they became local preachers and missionaries in the rural areas and also in some of the growing urban locations. Nor did they anticipate the startling new development that the Nederduitsche Gereformerde Sendingkerk (coloured), the Reformed Church of Africa (Indian) and the N. G. Kerk in Africa (African) would all opt for independence and become essentially nonracial. Liberal white Dutch Reformed Church members in some cases prefer to worship with racially integrated groups. These congregations are now speaking out courageously on social issues, to the discomfiture of their former mentors.

The white Dutch Reformed Churches have resisted "reform" and have retained their insulation, having refused since 1960 to participate in ecumenical bodies like the World Council of Churches and the South African Council of Churches. Earlier attempts to cooperate were shortlived when the DRC encountered criticism for their support of apartheid from their more liberal Protestant colleagues and for their ecumenicity from more conservative congregations. South African Calvinists even mistrust church leaders in Holland for their liberalism. They dismiss the growing protests of church people all over the world as "liberalists" insensitive to their social circumstance.

The coloured congregations were an anomaly because their leadership and rank-and-file membership spoke Afrikaans, and were culturally so close that they were often regarded as "brown Afrikaners". They too, however, were expected to retain separate congregations, churches, synods, and schools. Gradually white Dutch Reformed Church ministers were replaced by coloured preachers.

Conservative white Dutch Reformed Church leaders participate in the Broederbond (see Chapter 2), thus reinforcing the "political theology" of apartheid, mixing cultural preservation with religion. In 1945 Professor Cronje of the University of Pretoria wrote: "The racial policy which we as Afrikaners should promote must be directed to the preservation of racial and cultural variety. This is because it is according to the Will of God, and also because with the knowledge at our disposal, it can be justified on practical grounds . . . ." The rhetoric may have been modified of late, but not the practice. The reference to the Will of God is part of the Calvinist heritage of the Dutch Reformed Church. Afrikaners rely heavily on the Old Testament as well as on a Calvinist sense of mission or predestination. Some have identified themselves with the Children of Israel as the "chosen people" and with God's elect. They regard the survival and prosperity of their small groups as evidence of God's favor, and their electoral victories from 1948 to the present as mandates from God. As a "chosen people" they see themselves appointed to lead all of South Africa.

There have always been exceptions to these generalizations. Outstanding Afrikaners have left the church, often joining the newly independent, formerly "daughter" churches to oppose apartheid policies generally endorsed by their denomination. Although there are three major groups within the white Dutch Reformed Church, exhibiting distinct theological and cultural differences, their tendency to support the government is consistent. The purity of the faith had earlier been maintained through synodical church trials that condemned heresy where it arose. Sometimes this heresy seemed as much political as theological, but the judgment was usually made on a theological basis, and in most cases resulted in excommunication. In many of these instances it appeared that the congregations were more conservative than the top leadership. However, most white DRC leaders have felt constrained to go along with the membership.

> *The themes of rebellion and faith are as intertwined in the modern history of black South Africans as they are in the history of the dominant Afrikaner nationalists. So if the present deadly sparring between white and black nationalists in South Africa is to build into full-scale civil war that many on both sides now seem to anticipate, it will have to be a Christian civil war . . . .*
>
> Joseph Lelyveld, *New York Times Magazine,*
> March 14, 1982, p. 23.

## Other Religious Communities

Since the middle of the twentieth century a number of the Christian denominations inside South Africa have become more outspoken in their criticism of official policy especially at the upper leadership level. Some have moved toward mixed congregations, church services, and schools, though most are still far from integrated. Closer collaboration among churches with different ethnic traditions follows the experiences of considerable ecumenical cooperation in the creation of post-school institutions like Fort Hare University, Adams College, and the Federal Theological Seminary, all of which were taken over or otherwise threatened by the government when they appeared to be centers of radical student activity. The Seminary had to move, but is surviving. The Roman Catholic Church takes a strong position against apartheid. The Catholics have given up government subsidies and continue to operate integrated schools at their own expense.

Since mid-century the South African Council of Churches (SACC) has exercised growing influence, not only on ecumenicity but in coordinated efforts against apartheid. Most denominations, aside from the white DRC groups, either are members or, like the Roman Catholic Church, cooperate with its programs. In the 1970s and 1980s, leadership in the SACC has moved towards black churchmen. Bursaries (scholarships) aid promising scholars from all ethnic groups to continue their studies. Conferences and workshops are organized on religion and social issues. Publications provide stimulus to discussions in congregations and church schools. Current issues such as detentions, migratory labor, family life and nonviolent social change are addressed. The recognition of the rights of conscience has been fostered. Representations are made to authorities on religious and human issues. The current General Secretary, Bishop Desmond Tutu, has come under official attack for his outspoken criticism of apartheid. A legislative commission has been established to investigate the Council's finances, even though an outside auditor has cleared the organization of irregularities. A covertly subsidized competitor, the "Christian League," continues to harass the SACC. The AFSC has twice nominated Bishop Tutu for the Nobel Peace Prize in recognition of his courageous spiritual leadership for justice for his people.

> *"It's probably easy to forgive apartheid the tremendous pain it causes people economically and politically. But actually the most blasphemous thing about it is making a child of God doubt that he is a child of God. How much of who you have become has to be exorcised is incredible."*                    Bishop Tutu
>
> As quoted by Joseph Lelyveld, *New York Times Magazine,*
> March 14, 1982, p. 102.

The Christian Institute, now banned, is an example of an ecumenical, interracial church movement that inspired many Christians, especially younger ones, to vigorous, cooperative action opposing racial discimination. Both in its regional offices and nationally it published studies and inspirational messages for practical application. It stimulated political awareness throughout the country, and brought blacks and whites together in common endeavors.

Groups other than Christians have significant representation in South Africa. Only six per cent of the Indians are Christian; most of the others are Hindu. South Africans may be Muslim, Jew or Confucian. Such groups, plus those who claim no religious affiliation, make up 25% of the population. The other 75% classify themselves as Christian.

Persons of other than the Christian faith, particularly Hindus, have been active politically as individuals, though the organized religions of which they are a part have not. Many Jews in South Africa have opposed apartheid, thereby exposing themselves to latent anti-Semitism on the part of some Afrikaner nationalists, who may have carried it over from sympathy with Nazis during World War II. Israel's votes against apartheid in the UN have brought criticism in South Africa. Growing economic and trade cooperation, however, as well as a shared sense of being surrounded by hostile states, have brought South Africa and Israel closer together.

The only organized religious group anywhere in the world which supports apartheid is the white Dutch Reformed Church in South Africa.* The growing opposition of Christian Churches around the world to South African apartheid is described in Chapter 6.

## Quakers in South Africa

The Society of Friends has been active in the nineteenth and twentieth centuries in South Africa, although always with few members. Early nineteenth century British settlers in the Cape Province included some Quakers. Much later English Quakers developed commercial, business and humanitarian interests in the Transvaal and Natal provinces. Some Quakers came as educators.

One notable Friend was Richard Gush, who, like William Penn in Pennsylvania, maintained cordial and fair relations with the indigenous inhabitants from the time of his arrival in 1820. His memory and record are appreciated by many, including non-Quakers. The respect he won gave him the opportunity on occasion to halt or prevent hostilities between whites and blacks. He was recognized as a friend of the blacks, and he provided them food in times of hunger.

---

*For further details on religion in South Africa, see Marjorie Hope and James Young, *South African Churches in a Revolutionary Situation* (Maryknoll, N.Y.: Orbis Books, 1981).

A small British delegation of Quakers who visited in southern Africa before 1840 recognized the need for blacks and whites to have better facilities for living and working together. They raised special funds for the Lovedale Mission in the eastern Cape. It needed a better water system, so their funds created a "furrow" to conduct a stream from the Chiume (Tyiume) River to the Station. This has recently been replaced by a modernized system. The delegation established a Quaker Meeting for Worship in Cape Town in 1838, which functioned at least for the two years they were present, according to the journal of James Backhouse. Backhouse also founded a school for white and coloured children which was funded by English Friends and operated from 1840 to 1879. The present Meeting in Cape Town was started in 1903 and was approved by the London Yearly Meeting in 1906.

British Quakers' opposition to the Anglo-Boer War and their profound sympathy for the suffering of the Boer civilians is remembered in some of the Afrikaner patriotic museums. In this the Friends worked closely with Emily Hobhouse and her Anglican colleagues. The collection and return of many family Bibles, looted from Boer farms during the war and taken to England by soldiers, is still recalled with gratitude. The Bibles held vital family records as well as being important guides for the Boers' Christian piety. English Friends established and administered a relief fund which South African members also supported.

The Johannesburg Meeting for Worship began in 1912 in the YMCA; it was recognized by London Friends in 1917. The present-day Southern Africa Yearly Meeting includes groups in several adjacent countries and was formally organized in 1946. The South Africa General Meeting includes congregations and small groups gathering in various parts of the country. The Meeting in Soweto has grown slowly since the early 1960s.

Within South Africa itself there are today fewer than two hundred Quakers, mostly white and English-speaking. The Soweto Meeting is led by black members and draws black and white attenders. Considering the small number of Friends in South Africa and the relatively few black members, their activities are extensive. The Quaker Service Fund, which operates nonracially, is notably active in Johannesburg and the Cape, with especially elaborate and personalized activities on behalf of the country's black population who suffer political and economic injustice and for whom little exists in the way of general social services. The continued Quaker opposition to the evils and hardships of the apartheid system and to the militarization of the countryside is notable. They continue to seek recognition of the rights of conscientious objection to participation in war and of alternate nonmilitary forms of national service. Quakers, like many other Christian groups, tend to be fragmented and divided on some of these issues, but what they do is of considerable value. Friends are, however, the first to admit how limited their concerns and efforts can be, compared to the need. They are committed to a spiritual search for solutions to the social crises and agony which people from all ethnic backgrounds are undergoing.

In summary, this chapter has indicated some of the complexity of the South African scene. In spite of the antagonisms among the various ethnic groups who are aggravated by the official policy of apartheid and its "divide and rule" implications, there is a remarkable sense of love for the country among all groups. The bitter frustrations are real among the majority African population and, to a similar extent, among the smaller coloured and Indian groups. Their singular spirit and patience over the centuries may sometimes obscure their efforts at redress of their grievances. No history of the people of South Africa can be complete without some record of these efforts, which are discussed in the next chapter.

# CHAPTER 4

# *Amandla Ngawethu!*

"We shall not win our freedom except at the cost of great suffering, and we must be prepared to accept it."

Albert Luthuli, *Let My People Go,* p. 130.

Today in South Africa, in a barren hall or perhaps in an open field, the successor to the African herdsman of 1652 raises a clenched fist and shouts the Zulu word "Amandla!" (Power!). The audience raises a clenched fist and shouts the Zulu word "Ngawethu!" (is ours!). The recognition by Africans that power ultimately lies in their hands marks the beginning of the end of more than 325 years of white domination.

This chapter briefly examines the historical resistance by blacks to white domination, with greater attention given to the recent past and the present.

## 1652–1900

The Dutch East India Company's need to obtain a regular supply of fresh meat, fruit and vegetables for the trading post and for transient ships was met by enlarging the frontier community with settlers willing to farm. This action added to the conflict with Africans. There were cattle raids by settlers and by Africans. Six of the first fifteen years of the history of whites at the Cape were marked by what have come to be known as the Khoikhoi wars.

As the settlement extended east and north, displacing the Khoikhoi and the San, both Dutch and British whites came into conflict with more militant Africans, such as the Xhosa and the Zulu. The last twenty years of the eighteenth century were marked by frontier wars. Africans had neither guns nor horses. The superior technology of the whites gave them the major military victories, and they took the land by fire power.

In the first half of the nineteenth century, the last great warrior chieftans of the present South African area, Mzilikazi of the Matabele and Dingane (Dingaan, alternate spelling) of the Zulu, who ruled large territories and subjected many tribes, were helpless against the Boers' superior weapons. Mzilikazi and Dingane captured quantities of livestock and killed trekkers on the front edge of the invasion. Dingane killed a detachment of some seventy Boers led by Pieter Retief, but it was Dingane's troops which were slaughtered at Ncome River, renamed Blood River (Bloedriver in Afrikaans), December 16, 1838.

The Battle of Blood River in 1838 became a great myth in Afrikaner history. It was there that Afrikaners, faced with superior numbers of African warriors, promised God that if they won they would make a covenant with Him to hold this land for their posterity. Their superior firepower prevailed, and they interpreted their victory as God's will.

That battle marked the last military action large enough to be called warfare between the Afrikaners and the Africans until the current guerrilla war with SWAPO on the Namibian/Angolan border. The last annexation of African territory was that of Pondoland in 1894.

The period 1652-1900 was a time when southern Africa was torn with many violent conflicts. Africans were striving for territorial control over other Africans, while at the same time trying to hold back the advance of whites. Whites were battling whites as British and Boers fought for control, while both fought the Africans. There was conflict among groups on all sides.

By 1900 it was not clear which group of whites would win, but it was clear that the Africans had lost to superior technology, but the military defeat by whites and loss of land did not turn them into racists. White missionaries continued to operate in the territories of African leaders such as Moshweshwe, Khama, Mzilikazi and Dingane through all of their reigns, and friendly personal relationships were maintained.

## 1900-1950

At the turn of the century, resistance against white domination took a new form. After 250 years of unsuccessful war, blacks turned to techniques of petition, negotiation and nonviolent direct action. Social action seldom fits neatly into time compartments, and there was overlap between the nineteenth and the twentieth centuries as tactics were shifted. Mahatma Gandhi arrived in South Africa in 1893 and was soon involved in a petition campaign, South Africa's first, which resulted in ten thousand signatures protesting the removal of Asians from the voters' roll in Natal. The campaign was successful. In 1894, Gandhi founded the Natal Indian Congress to continue to press for Indian rights.

In a small military action in 1906, the Zulu rebellion led by Chief Bambata in Natal was quickly crushed. Gandhi recruited a medical unit of Indians to treat injured Zulus, a task refused by whites.

The beginnings of African nationalism and political organization, like the resistance of the Indian community, date back to the late nineteenth century. One African organization, Imbumba Yama Afrika, is sometimes called the seed of the African National Congress. It was formed in 1882 in the Eastern Cape, where in 1884 the first African political newspaper was also started, with John Tengo Jabavu as editor. Early African political activity in the Cape was the result of the qualified franchise in that province. There were Africans able to meet the qualifications, which were economic rather than racial. Political activity of both Africans and coloureds tended to be an adjunct to white political activity.

The period between the Peace of Vereeniging in 1902, which ended the Anglo–Boer War, and the approval of Union in 1910, which established the current South African state, set the context within which most African political organization and activity germinated. There was a general dissatisfaction among blacks that the Peace of Vereeniging created no rights for them and failed to protect even the limited rights they already had.

Organizations which came into being at that time included the African Political Organization, the Transvaal National Natives Union, the Cape Native Congress, the Orange River Colony Native Congress, the Natal Native Congress, the Transvaal Native Vigilance Association, the Transvaal British Indian Association, the Basuto Committee, the Native Congress (Transvaal), the Native Electoral Association and the South African Native Convention.

Of these, the African Political Organization, with members in the Cape, Natal and the Orange Free State, was the first national black resistance group. It was started by coloureds but also had African members.

*Imvo Zabantsundu,* Jabavu's newspaper, printed a petition to King Edward VII in 1905 from the members of the Native United Political Association of the Transvaal Colony together with the Natives of that Colony, protesting anti-African legislation.

At the time of the negotiations for formation of the Union of South Africa, the South African Native Convention met to petition for "full and equal rights and privileges without distinction of class, colour or creed." The Convention's position went farther toward equality than the African Political Organization, which asked only for political rights for all "fully civilized" people. Neither petition was successful.

African nationalism in South Africa is often identified as beginning with the formation of the Union of South Africa in 1910. Blacks began then to seek a majority-ruled state in opposition to white domination, although it would be many years before nationalism was articulated in that way.

With the failure to win rights in the agreement of Union and a general deteriorating political situation for blacks in all of the four provinces, the South African Native National Congress was founded in 1912. The name was changed to African National Congress in 1923. The ANC is the oldest of all African liberation groups. Albert Luthuli, long-time ANC leader and a Nobel Peace Prize winner in 1960, said the business of the ANC is "to right the total exclusion of the African from the management of South Africa, to give direction to the forces of liberation, to harness peacefully the growing resistance to continued oppression, and, by various nonviolent means, to demand the redress of injustice.''

In today's context, when the South African government credits the Communists for every effort at black political advancement, it is important to see how much African effort and political organization was invested in the struggle for equality before the Communist Party was born. The resistance was expressed not only through 250 years of armed conflict, but also through decades of organization. The Communist Party of South Africa was founded in 1921, and it made racial equality a major part of its agenda. However, the Communists were often openly critical of the ANC, which would not add communism to its agenda.

## Role of the Church

The main contribution of the church in the struggle against apartheid is probably not in corporate political and social action but rather in the education of the leaders and members of African nationalist organizations. The Oxford History of South Africa reports that it was educated Christians, attracted to Western culture, who initiated the movement to African nationalism, and shaped its ideology.*

At first only the church offered education to Africans. Lovedale, one of the better known missionary institutions, opened in 1841. By 1896, 3,448 African students had attended Lovedale. It was one of five or six mission schools in which the first African doctors, lawyers, editors and political leaders received their education. Fort Hare, founded in 1916, was the first church-established college in all of southern Africa, attracting some of the political leaders of surrounding countries. Robert Mugabe and Simon Muzenda of Zimbabwe, for example, got their first higher education there. Joshua Nkomo attended another church-established school in South Africa, Adams College in Natal.

At the same time, church groups were sending Africans out of the country for higher education. The Natal Native Affairs Commissioner's report of 1906–07 estimated that at least 150 Africans were in the U.S. for study. There were probably more in Britain and a scattering in other countries. A recent survey of personnel resources for the new state of Zimbabwe gave an estimate of 16,000 college graduates. South African graduates come from a country four times the size of Zimbabwe, with an education infrastructure that developed earlier and provided more national opportunities for higher education. South Africa clearly has many more graduates than Zimbabwe. The memberships of ANC, PAC, the Black Consciousness Movement and

---

*Leonard Thompson and Monica Wilson, *The Oxford History of South Africa* (Oxford: The Clarendon Press, 1971).

labor unions has grown beyond the pool of educated Christians. But the latter group still provides the major part of the leadership for resistance to white domination.

The first leadership in institutional separation from white domination also came from the church through the movement known as Ethiopian Churches. Some of these churches were established by the African Methodist Episcopal Church, an American black-organized church. Other churches came from schisms within mission churches. The first Ethiopian Church in South Africa was founded in 1892.

## Help Sought Outside

At the turn of the century Africans were using a new technique of resistance: seeking political help from outside the country. Africans were successful in getting support from members of the British Parliament and others in the negotiations at the time of Union in 1910, but these British were as powerless in securing African rights as were the Africans themselves.

Delegations of Africans were sent to London in 1914 and again in 1919 to seek help from the Crown. Although those within the four provinces of South Africa received no help, Africans in Swaziland, Basutoland (now Lesotho) and Bechuanaland (now Botswana) were able to convince the Crown that they should not become part of South Africa. These three former protectorates are now independent countries.

At the beginning of the century Indians led by Gandhi were also petitioning Britain for assistance in gaining their rights in South Africa. They asked for and received some help from India in pleading their cause, then and again later. At that time Indian and African resistance and protest were separate, even when parallel action was underway.

After World War II the United Nations provided the structure for outside assistance against apartheid. Most of the nations of the world saw the protest against apartheid as a valid concern for the UN from the beginning. By the late 1950s, the U.S. had conceded that racial discrimination in South Africa was an appropriate matter for UN consideration. After the Sharpeville Massacre in 1960 Britain finally joined the rest of the world in seeing apartheid as more than an internal matter for South Africa.

## Mahatma Gandhi in South Africa

Mahatma Gandhi spent two periods of his life in South Africa. From 1893 to 1900 he led the petition campaign and organized the Natal Indian Congress. In 1901 he left South Africa to establish himself as a barrister in Bombay, but within a few months he received an urgent plea to return to South Africa, this time to the Transvaal. By early 1903 he had returned.

The immediate problem to be confronted was an anti-Indian immigration law, but more threatening was a growing anti-Indian attitude on the part of Transvaal officialdom. Soon after his arrival, Gandhi said, "I could see that the Asiatic Department was merely a frightful engine of oppression for Indians."

The immigration law continued to be a matter of concern throughout Gandhi's time in South Africa, but the "Black Act," as the Indians called an Asian registration law proposed in 1906, soon took priority. This law called for registration and fingerprinting of all Asian men and women. Registration certificates would be required to obtain licenses to trade and other essentials from the Transvaal. Failure to register would result in imprisonment. In an irony of colonial operations the law was disallowed in 1906 by Britain, but when the Transvaal obtained responsible government status on January 1 of the following year British approval of the legislation became automatic. In 1907 the Transvaal's first measure passed was the budget, the second was the Asiatic Registration Act.

Indian resentment of the forceful fingerprinting of women was so strong that women were omitted from registration, but the bill had no other changes from the original proposal. The Gandhian-led Indian response, first suggested by other Indian leaders, was a massive nonregistration campaign. It was within the context of this campaign that Gandhi coined the word *Satyagraha*. He rejected the term "passive resistance," although he approved "nonviolence" as an English equivalent. More specifically, Gandhi translated *Satyagraha* as "force which is truth and love" and also as "soul-force." Physical force was totally rejected against either persons or property.

Many were arrested for nonregistration, and Gandhi was among them. The campaign was called off when he thought he had worked out a compromise for voluntary registration and repeal of the law. When it became clear that General Smuts, then head of the Transvaal government, would not honor the agreement, the Indians held a mass protest, climaxed by a bonfire to destroy the voluntary certificates they had already obtained. The Indians wrote Smuts of their intent in advance; his reponse as reported in the press seems to have set the pattern for South African government leaders over the years: "I am sorry that some agitators are trying to inflame poor Indians who will be ruined if they succumb to their blandishments."

The Transvaal also passed a discriminatory immigration law in 1907 and jailed and deported Indians for refusing to comply with both the registration and immigration laws. Some Indians, imprisoned in the Diepkloof Convict Prison with a jailor who insulted them, pioneered with a hunger strike. After seven days they were transferred to another prison, an alternative they said would be acceptable if the jailor could not be removed.

On March 14, 1913 a judge in the Cape Supreme Court ruled that the only legal marriages in South Africa were those performed by the Christian rites and registered by the Registrar of Marriages. This invalidated most Indian marriages, as few Indians were Christians. Gandhi's effort to get legislative relief was unsuccessful. *Satyagrahis,* including women for the first time, entered illegally into the Transvaal and sold goods on the streets without a license, seeking arrest to protest the nullification of their marriages. At first the women were not arrested, but by September and October groups of both men and women, who would leave the territory and then reenter illegally, were arrested and sentenced to three months in prison. Meanwhile, a head tax on some Indian laborers was added to the list of grievances.

The final protest was a march by Gandhi with 1,037 men, 127 women and 57 children into the Transvaal. They started out on November 6, 1913 and twice en route Gandhi was arrested and released on bond. On a third arrest he was sentenced to jail for nine months. The marchers were deported to Natal in three trains. In Natal they were sent to jail, then moved to a coal mine, where they refused to work. Not surprisingly, supporting strikes developed among other Indian workers.

In the course of negotiations with Smuts, all issues were eventually settled to the satisfaction of the Indians. Gandhi then felt free to return to India in July 1914. He wrote, "Our victory was implicit in our combination of the two qualities on nonviolence and determination."

As Gandhi's work drew the attention of Africans, cooperation began between the Natal Indian Congress and the ANC. His work in South Africa is, however, primarily of historical interest for it was here that he worked through some of his ideas and tested them successfully in a few limited campaigns. Ironically, it is Gandhi's work in India which had significant impact on the thinking of African leaders. Albert Luthuli became a convert to Gandhi's methods. Other African leaders such as Kenneth Kaunda, now President of Zambia; Robert Sobukwe, founder of the Pan Africanist Congress; Steve Biko, leader of the Black Consciousness Movement; Chief Gatsha Buthelezi, head of Inkatha and KwaZulu; and Robert Mugabe, Prime Minister of Zimbabwe, acknowledge Gandhi's influence on their ideas.

### Other Pre-1950 Resistance

Africans organized and led nonviolent actions of resistance in the period before 1950. In 1913, for example, African women in the Orange Free State held off the extension of pass laws to them by refusing to carry passes. In 1943 a bus boycott in the African township of Alexandra was provoked by a fare increase, nineteen years ahead of the Montgomery, Alabama boycott.

A 1919 ANC anti-pass campaign resulted in 500 arrests in Johannesburg. Also in that city, among the first strikes in South Africa were those of African sanitation workers in 1918. Four hundred dockers struck in Cape Town in 1919, and some 40,000 African miners struck in 1920.

Three Africans were killed by police in a pass-burning demonstration in 1930. African women organized nonviolent resistance against curfew regulations in the Transvaal in 1932.

In 1943, the most massive African strike included over 70,000 min-workers, nine of whom were killed by police. Another strike in 1946 was broken by police.

The Indians remembered some of Gandhi's lessons. Six hundred Indians were jailed in Natal in 1944 in their resistance against segregation. Nearly 2,000 Indians (and a few whites, including Rev. Michael Scott) were jailed in Natal for nonviolent resistance to anti-Indian legislation. Blacks continued organizing and promoting political action, in addition to demonstrations. The nationwide South African Indian Congress was formed in 1926, and with evidence of some impatience with their elders, younger members of the ANC formed the Congress Youth League in 1944.

After World War II, Dr. A. B. Xuma, ANC leader, published a popular book entitled *African Claims,* in which he applied the ideals of the Atlantic Charter to South Africa.

For South African blacks, the first half of the twentieth century was a time of facing up to the reality of white domination. Laws were getting more restrictive against all blacks. At the same time, there was some hope that organization, petition, good will and logic might make some inroads on the obvious injustices.


## 1950–1975

The third quarter of the twentieth century brought increasing oppression, with the government putting more and more of their resources into main-taining the status quo by force. It was also a time of mounting resistance on the part of blacks. When the Group Areas Act was passed in 1950, the ANC sponsored a mass labor strike in Transvaal townships. Police opened fire on a crowd of protestors killing eighteen and wounding thirty.

The first nationwide campaign of resistance, the Defiance Against Unjust Laws Campaign, was planned in 1951 and launched in 1952 with remarkable success during its first four months. The campaign was organized by the ANC with the Indian Congress participating. Its leaders had developed a nonviolent strategy which would dramatize the injustice of the laws by accepting arrest for violating those laws. The authorities would be notified of the time and place of each act of civil disobedience. In the whole campaign more than 8,000 persons were arrested, among them Gandhi's son and a few whites. Crowds of over 10,000 attended open meetings at Cape Town, Port Elizabeth, East London, Pretoria and Durban on June 26, 1952, and for the first time, the white press gave almost daily coverage to the campaign. ANC membership increased from 7,000 to 100,000. Although Nelson Mandela was the key figure in implementation of this campaign, Albert Luthuli was nominally in charge of the operation, and the government Native Affairs Department deposed him from his chieftainship because of it. Eventually, Luthuli was restricted to his home village.

After four months of highly disciplined nonviolent action, rioting broke out in Port Elizabeth, Johannesburg, Kimberley and East London. At least forty persons were killed, and there was extensive property damage. The riots ended the Defiance Campaign. Luthuli and the ANC charged that *agents provocateurs* were responsible for starting the riots, an accusation with which most informed, outside observers of South Africa agree. In his autobiography Luthuli concludes, "The prospect before the white supremacists, if they were going to react to our challenge in a civilized way, was that arrests would continue indefinitely. Behind the thousands already arrested there were more, many more. The challenge of nonviolence was more than they could meet. It robbed them of the initiative." Therefore, Luthuli reports, violence was initiated by the police to create the riots and restore initiative to whites.

## Resistance Spreads

In spite of its untimely and unfortunate end, the Defiance Campaign served notice on South African whites that African resistance had to be taken seriously. After the Campaign, Julius Lewin, a noted South African lecturer on African law, pointed out in the *Political Quarterly* (London, 1953) that "the first effect of undermining Congress was to strengthen those less responsible and less reasonable groups in African life that have begun to preach enmity against all white people as such, and perhaps to toy with the idea of terrorism as a technique for securing political change." Lewin was right, missing only the point that it would be the African National Congress itself who would feel forced to undertake that kind of action which its opponents called terrorism. Lewin (a man his fellow white South Africans should have taken more seriously) also pointed out that "there are no moderate African leaders" in South African government terms. The real leaders were already at a more radical level than was acceptable to the government.

The Defiance Campaign ended, but resistance continued with many sponsors in addition to the ANC. As Luthuli reported, "Throughout the country as a whole resistance was uncoordinated and haphazard. But it was there, and it arose out of the whites' refusal to share the country with us, or to permit us to walk free in our own land."

Resistance has always been varied and sometimes haphazard in South Africa. There are many, many examples to report.

In Namibia in 1924 a hundred Khoikhoi were killed in the course of refusing to pay a dog tax.

In the first of many protests against the Bantu Education Act of 1953, a school boycott sponsored by ANC in 1955 resulted in 100,000 students staying home.

In 1956 thousands of African women took to the streets protesting the extension of pass laws to women. The police responded with force. Three women were killed. Women are still required to carry passes.

In 1955 the vision of an egalitarian South Africa was articulated by representatives of all races in the adoption of the Freedom Charter by 3,000 delegates meeting in an open field at Kliptown. The Freedom Charter, still a basic manifesto for ANC, declares South Africa belongs to all of its people. "Every man and woman shall have the right to vote for and stand as candidate for all bodies which make laws." As a cooperative effort by ANC, the Congress of Democrats and a number of other groups, the adoption of the Freedom Charter was a high point in the life of the soon to decline Congress Alliance.

> *We, the people of South Africa, declare for all our country and the world to know; that South Africa belongs to all who live in it, black and white, and that no government can justly claim authority unless it is based on the will of all the people; that our people have been robbed of their birthright to land, liberty and peace by a form of government founded on injustice and inequality; that our country will never be prosperous or free until all our people live in brotherhood, enjoying equal rights and opportunities; that only a democratic state, based on the will of all the people can secure to all their birthright without distinction of colour, race, sex or belief. . . .*
>
> *from the Freedom Charter of South Africa adopted in June 1955 at a conference convened by the ANC & others.*

Robert Sobukwe broke with the ANC in 1958 to organize the Pan Africanist Congress, a new liberation group emphasizing black unity and leadership which provided a new focal point for resistance. The first big action by PAC was a nonviolent demonstration against passes in 1960. What has come to be known as the Sharpeville Massacre was one result, with 70 Africans killed and 186 wounded by South African forces. Many were shot in the back as they fled from the scene. In the following three weeks there were massive demonstrations, marches, gatherings and pass burnings across the country. There were thousands of arrests, and the South African government passed its 90-day detention law as a new repressive measure.

## A Transition Point in Attitudes

Sharpeville marks a clear transition point in the attitude of South African blacks on the tactics of liberation. There had long been a division between those committed solely to nonviolent action and those who thought nonviolence was not enough by itself. After Sharpeville, there was a coming together almost unanimously to the view that violence is necessary to win liberation for South African blacks.

Late in 1961 ANC members, including some members of the Communist Party, formed Umkonto We Sizwe ("Spear of the Nation" in Zulu) to carry out sabotage. The group included Africans, Indians and whites. December 16 is the Day of the Covenant, a "holy day" in South Africa for Afrikaners commemorating the victory at Blood River. On that day in 1961 the group placed bombs in Johannesburg and Port Elizabeth aimed at destroying property, not persons. In the following eighteen months until they were captured, they claimed more than seventy acts of sabotage. Sabotage activity under the name Spear of the Nation continues.

A short-lived violent, antiwhite creation of the PAC, called "Poqo" (Xhosa for "alone"), was crushed and most of its known leaders executed. Poqo was the forerunner of APLA (Azanian People's Liberation Army), another creation of PAC.

In spite of the acceptance of violence as necessary by many Africans, liberation leaders agree that nonviolence is a satisfactory complement to violent protest or guerrilla warfare. In 1961, the year after Sharpeville, ANC attempted to organize a three-day nationwide strike in protest of a "white only" referendum. The government countered with massive action and the strike had only limited success.

## Black Consciousness

In 1969 the South African Students' Organization (SASO) split from the nonracial but white-led National Union of South African Students (NUSAS) and from the University Christian Movement. The president of SASO was Steve Biko, who thought that Africans must provide their own leadership for liberation. Even though NUSAS was already seen by the government as a subversive organization, Biko did not feel that NUSAS could meet the need of blacks. SASO quickly won African, coloured and Indian student support. Marxists were critical of SASO for, as they saw it, failing to understand the class struggle.

In 1970 Biko became a leading exponent of the Black Consciousness Movement for promoting the SASO idea of black leadership, much like the Black Power movement in the U.S. Related organizations included the Black Peoples Convention (BPC). The BPC immediately ruled out all cooperation with homeland leaders and government institutions. Black Community Programs (BCP) was supported by the South African Council of Churches and the Christian Institute. High school and primary students formed the South African Student Movement (SASM) in Soweto, and similar groups were organized elsewhere.

In September 1974 SASO and BPC defied a ban and held a "Viva Frelimo" rally in Durban and at the University of the North to celebrate the liberation of Mozambique. Many blacks were arrested at both rallies, and nine leaders were charged. Over the two years of their trial the defendants often entered the courtroom singing freedom songs or giving the black power salute and shout. The defendants were finally given five- and six-year sentences. The news media kept the public informed of the trial action.

In December 1974 the Black Renaissance Convention met. More than 300 African, coloured and Asian participants were brought together by Catholic and Protestant leaders. This group of intellectuals, considered moderates, discussed black consciousness ideas. The convention called for a united, democratic South Africa with one person, one vote and an equitable distribution of wealth. It also called for foreign countries to withdraw cultural, educational and economic support from "the existing racist government and all its racist institutions."

A major impact on resistance in 1971 was the strike of African workers in Namibia. Most whites thought that these mostly illiterate workers were incapable of organization. The strike was widespread and brought some improvement for the workers. This strike encouraged others and was probably a factor in the governmental overhaul of labor laws.

Black dockworkers followed with a strike in Durban in 1972. Fifteen workers lost their jobs, but a pay increase was won. The next year there were strikes in Durban, Cape Town, and Hammersdale with mixed results. But black labor was moving to the front as another power for resistance. All of these strikes of the early 1970s were illegal, but at that time the government seemed unable to deal with them by the usual law and order methods.

## 1975-1982

The years since 1975 have been filled with black resistance and government counteraction in South Africa. Sharpeville, the rash of strikes, and the Black Consciousness Movement set the context for the Soweto rebellion and its aftermath. A youth crusade shook South Africa as the 1976 Soweto demonstration grew into the third nationwide protest action. On June 16, 1976 twenty thousand students in Soweto, an African township with a population of nearly two million, started a peaceful march toward a protest meeting to be held in Orlando stadium. The protest was organized to object to a longstanding but newly enforced government ruling that one-half of all high school subjects were to be taught in Afrikaans instead of English. The South African Student Movement (SASM) had organized the meeting. The students were in good spirits and carried signs indicating the nonviolent nature of the protest. Before they reached the stadium they were confronted by police. It is unclear whether the students threw stones first or the police fired first, but the police fired into the unarmed crowd of youngsters. The first to be killed was a thirteen-year-old boy. The picture of him being carried out of action has become a powerful symbol for the Soweto uprising.

The Bantu Education Act had already been the object of sporadic protest since its inception in 1953. Afrikaans, as the language of their officials and those seen as the primary oppressors, was seen as the language of oppression. Students had been highly politicized by the Black Consciousness Movement. Police action in Soweto was the spark that set off nationwide protest. Before the protests were over, between seven hundred and a thousand were killed, including fifty coloureds. More than five thousand persons were injured. Two whites were beaten to death in Soweto on the first day of the rebellion. There were other isolated cases of white deaths, but their number remained small, probably not more than six in all. Typically, the cost of white supremacy is paid in black corpses.

Many post-Soweto demonstrations were nonviolent, but there was also widespread destruction of government property in African townships. Soweto hardened the belief of blacks that violence is necessary to end South African oppression. An estimated ten thousand students left the country for guerrilla training or education as a result of Soweto. Conversations were held with some of these students in Botswana in 1977 by the participants in the American Friends Service Committee study tour of the Frontline States. It was the students' opinion that violence was necessary for the liberation of South Africa. Some South African students are receiving formal education in Botswana, but no guerrilla training is done in that country.

In addition to hardening attitudes on the use of violence, Soweto and its aftermath shifted the focus of resistance to a younger generation and more dispersed leadership. Some older generation leaders had to run rapidly to catch up with those they thought they led. Protests by youth in South Africa have never completely stopped since 1976. There were widespread school boycotts again in 1980 and 1981 involving blacks, coloureds and Asians.

The death of Steve Biko while in police custody (see Chapter 2) touched off wide protests in 1977. Again the ground had been well prepared, for in addition to consciousness-raising by the Black Consciousness Movement, Steve Biko's violent death was the forty-fourth death of a political prisoner in police custody within fifteen years. Some of these prisoners "jumped" out of windows; some were found hanging in their cells; some were listed "cause of death unknown."

The protest in reaction to Steve Biko's death brought heavy-handed response from the South African government. Seventeen Black Consciousness organizations and the Christian Institute were banned. *The World*, a white-owned but black-edited newspaper, was closed down. Percy Qoboza, editor of the *World*, and Dr. Motlana, chairman of the Committee of Ten, a Soweto leadership group growing out of the Soweto rebellion, were detained. Seven whites well known for their work for racial equality were banned, including two Afrikaners, Beyers Naude, founder of the Christian

Institute and Theo Kotze, director of the Institute in Cape Town. Donald Woods, editor of the *East London Daily Dispatch*, was also banned. Kotze and Woods have left South Africa and Beyers Naude, still banned, was one of several who were seen by representatives of the AFSC visiting South Africa in August 1980.

Some indication of the continued tempo of resistance is indicated by the following table:

Prosecutions from July 1, 1978 to June 30, 1979 under the Internal Security Act

| | |
|---|---:|
| Public violence | 1,130 |
| Unlawful & riotous assembly | 253 |
| Sabotage | 86 |
| Intent to racial unrest | 23 |
| Malicious damage to property | 16,283 |
| Arson | 1,059 |
| Obstructing | 221 |
| | 19,055 |

South African Institute of Race Relations (SAIRR), *1980 Survey of Race Relations*, p. 246.

If a proportionate number of Americans were prosecuted for security violations, it would mean nearly 200,000 prosecutions per year.

## Resistance in the 1980s

The South African government, the South Africa Foundation, and some U.S. corporations together spend millions of dollars in the United States each year to present South Africa as a pleasant, quiet country, safe for profitable investment and delightful tourism. It is sometimes noted that there are occasional racial incidents and political protests, but no more than might be expected in the United States or elsewhere.

To give a well documented picture of internal resistance to South African policy, the balance of this section presents incidents culled from a single source, the *1980 Survey of Race Relations in South Africa*, published by the South African Institute of Race Relations, an impeccable source of information with decades of experience. The SAIRR *Survey* does not claim to report every incident of protest or unrest, since there are many incidents of unrest too small to appear in the newspapers or get into statistical reports. Incidents such as blacks being moved from white beaches without arrests (and there were many such incidents) are not cited. The Institute reports that during 1980 "the country experienced the most sustained period of unrest since 1976." Statistics on unrest constitute a minor part of the SAIRR work, making up little more than 1% of the 690 pages of annual report. Our categories are those used by the Institute. This listing is included to give a cumulative impact on readers in the U.S. who are not accustomed to such pervasive police activity and public violence.

## Meeting Ban

On April 1, 1980 the ban on outdoor gatherings was extended for one year, as has been done each year since 1976. Sporting events are excepted, and permission for outdoor meetings can be given by the Minister of Justice or a magistrate. Some indication of what such a ban means over a twelve month period is shown by the following examples:

1. The Chief Magistrate of Johannesburg refused an application by residents of two African townships to march to Johannesburg city hall in protest of rent increases.

2. Permission to hold a meeting in Soweto to discuss dissatisfaction with the community council was refused.

3. In Nkowankowa Township all open air gatherings of more than two people were banned following student demonstrations.

4. Thirty-one persons, including two journalists, were arrested at the unveiling of a tombstone of an executed urban guerrilla.

5. At one school boycott 714 pupils, age twelve and older, were arrested. Thousands were arrested across South Africa in related boycotts.

6. A Free Mandela rally at the University of Natal was banned just minutes before it was due to start. A substitute rally was also banned.

7. Fort Hare University banned all mass meetings.

8. Bishop Tutu and fifty-three others, mostly priests, were arrested when they marched in protest against the detention of Rev. John Thorne.

9. Although not prosecuted, 130 African children were arrested when they marched to the Grahamstown police station to show solidarity with twelve arrested youths.

10. In Uitenhage 275 pupils were arrested when they marched from Kwanobuhle Township to town.

11. There were widespread bans on all meetings in June to prevent commemoration of those who died in the Soweto rebellion of June 1976. All political meetings of more than ten persons were banned until the end of August in much of the country.

12. The chief magistrate of Grahamstown prohibited funerals and burial services in black townships for one weekend in August because of confrontations with police at previous funerals.

13. In parts of Cape Town a ban on public outdoor gatherings was extended for two years from August 12, 1980. Religious and sporting events were not exempted.

14. In Port Elizabeth, all meetings to commemorate the death of Steve Biko were banned for September 13-14.

15. All public meetings were banned by Lebowa for the weekends of October 11–12 and 18–19 to prevent meetings set by the Azanian People's Organization (AZAPO), a Black Consciousness Movement group.

## Civil Unrest Over Soweto Anniversary

The following are incidents of civil unrest growing out of the 1980 commemoration of the Soweto deaths in 1976:

1. On June 15 the police used teargas, batons and sneeze gas to disperse several hundred people gathered outside a church in Soweto to commemorate the Soweto deaths. The meeting set for inside the church had been banned.

2. In a similar situation in Mfuleni Township on the same day, a police constable was stabbed to death during a baton charge.

3. Crowds were dispersed the next day in Soweto and Diepkloof, with one person killed. Several youths were injured by batons during house to house searches for participants.

4. In Noordgesig, a coloured township, seventeen youths were shot after allegedly looting a shop and stoning vehicles and buses.

5. In Bloemfontein, five persons were shot when police fired birdshot and plastic bullets to disperse the crowd.

6. Tear gas was used to disperse a group of four hundred youths in Port Elizabeth.

7. In Kwa Thema, Springs, 210 persons were arrested when they broke into a Dutch Reformed Church to hold a commemorative service.

8. In Kwa Mashu, Durban, police dispersed a crowd of school children with tear gas after the children set up road obstacles and stoned buses.

9. On June 17 in Elsies River in Cape Town, 25 persons were reported killed and 150 injured as shops were gutted and cars burned. Reinforcements of antiriot police were flown into Cape Town. Arson continued for several days. Many Cape residents protested the disregard by the police for human life.

10. On the same day in the Boland, one person was shot and others injured when petrol bombs were thrown at the Paarl East police station. Two schools were set on fire and eight businesses looted.

11. On June 18 arson and looting on the Cape Flats continued, with police using guns. Hospitals were instructed not to release figures on numbers of dead and wounded, and the police also refused to release them.

12. Police used tear gas and batons to disperse students at the University of Durban–Westville following stone throwing. One hundred students and three policemen were treated for injuries.

## Other Civil Unrest in 1980

Additional examples of civil unrest include the following:

1. In February at the funeral of one of the guerrillas killed in the bank siege at Silverton, police used tear gas to disperse two hundred mourners who stoned buses and cars.

2. On March 9 at the funeral of another guerrilla, attended by ten thousand people, police used tear gas, batons and sjamboks to prevent the hijacking of motor vehicles.

3. On July 15 Violet Tsili was shot by police in the yard of her house near a school where pupils had been dispersed with tear gas and batons. Fifteen thousand persons attended her funeral. Police used birdshot and tear gas to disperse stone-throwing crowds afterwards. Boy-Boy Nobiba was also killed.

4. At Nobiba's funeral, three men were killed by police after their armored vehicle was attacked with petrol bombs. Beer halls, schools and shops were burned.

5. On the weekend of July 26–27 police fired birdshot to disperse crowds in Kwazakhele in Port Elizabeth after a bus was set on fire and police patrols stoned.

6. On August 7 police fired birdshot and arrested some students when four thousand marched from Diepkloof schools in protest against Bantu education and increased rents.

7. On August 11–14 in Nyanga and Crossroads, Western Cape, there were stonings and arson incidents accompanied by police use of birdshot and tear gas. Four persons were killed.

8. On August 18–20 police used tear gas and birdshot to disperse crowds in Fort Beaufort. One young woman was killed.

9. There were stonings and arson in Port Elizabeth on August 24–25. Police fired birdshot to disperse youths trying to burn an overturned police van.

10. Police clashed in Seshego on August 25 with students boycotting classes and stoning vehicles.

11. Unrest, particularly stoning of vehicles continued during September and October in Cape Town and Eastern Cape.

12. On the weekend of October 25–26 two children in Guguletu were killed by police shots fired at stone-throwing crowds during celebration of Mike Weaver's boxing victory over Gerrie Coetzee.

13. On September 11 in Sada, a Ciskei policeman was stoned to death and a student shot during school unrest.

14. On November 6 four persons were killed and 16 wounded in Port Elizabeth as police fired birdshot at crowds throwing stones.

15. Tear gas, batons and rubber bullets were used by police in Soweto on October 15 to disperse crowds protesting rent increases and a visit to Soweto

by Dr. Koornhof, Minister of Cooperation and Development.

16. A police baton charge in Soweto broke up a commemoration service for banned organizations on October 19.

17. In the course of a bus boycott over fare increases in the Cape, there was a great deal of violence. Nearly 150 buses were stoned and two drivers injured on June 2–3. On June 11 petrol bombs were thrown at buses. Twenty persons were arrested on June 12 when a bus was stoned and there were alleged attempts at the forceful removal of passengers. Pirate (unlicensed) taxi drivers carrying boycotters were arrested.

### Strikes

Information is becoming available on the total number of strikes and the number of black workers involved in strikes in 1980. Antero Pietila of the Johannesburg Bureau of the *Baltimore Sun* reported in the *Sun* (May 25, 1981) that there were 207 "illegal job actions" in 1980, twice the number in 1979, and that 1981 would show an increase over 1980. Strikes in South Africa are increasingly becoming a way of demonstrating black power. During the latter part of 1981 and early in 1982, the government's concern about strikes increased and several hundred union leaders were detained. The strikes are usually illegal. Listed here are a few examples of strikes in 1980 which involved police action.

1. On April 25 at an apple cooperative strike of Africans and coloureds, police were called in, and they made forty arrests. Strikers eventually gained some of their objectives in a new agreement, including a 50% pay increase for the lowest paid workers.

2. On May 22 a strike began in a textile mill which eventually involved nearly seven thousand workers. Seven leaders were charged under the Riotous Assemblies Act, and 298 were charged with taking part in a strike. Not all strikers were rehired but small wage increases were gained. A meeting of workers with the liaison committee was banned.

3. On June 16 more than three thousand Volkswagen workers walked out. A meeting to inform workers of the outcome of national wage negotiations was banned under the Riotous Assemblies Act. The strike spread through related industries with wages the overt issue. Police were active in dispersing workers.

4. The Johannesburg municipal workers' strike started with six hundred workers on July 24 and grew to ten thousand in less than a week. Two leaders were charged under the Sabotage Act, which has a maximum penalty of death and a minimum penalty of five years in prison. Lesser charges were substituted later. More than fifteen hundred workers lost their jobs. 185 workers were sent back to the homelands.

5. On May 19 about eight hundred meat packers were on strike in Cape Town. Forty-two workers were convicted of being in the city illegally after

being fired. Workers were prevented from meeting by a ban under the Riotous Assemblies Act. The strike failed after three months of effort.

6. Two hundred workers were fired by National Converter Industries in a union recognition dispute. The entire workforce was locked out. Police arrested 128 workers outside the factory gates. All those arrested were convicted in East London under the Riotous Assemblies Act and fined.

7. On August 6 police wielding batons charged 250 workers in a Royalite Batteries factory canteen in East London. All workers were charged with having staged a sit-in strike and were dismissed. Security police visited the homes of 58 strikers.

Strikes, often starting peacefully but ending in violence, continue in South Africa. From July 1 to July 3, 1982 in four gold mines not far from Johannesburg a strike by African miners became a riot, resulting in eight African deaths, six of them from police bullets. Mining is one of the higher paid occupations for Africans. The average African miner is paid $216 a month while the average white miner earns $1,080 a month.*

## Security Trials

There were thirty-two security trials in South Africa in 1980 in which the defendants, if found guilty, would be liable for the death penalty. Here are five examples of major trials:

1. Nine members of ANC were charged with high treason in the Pretoria Supreme Court. The defendants, all Africans, were aged 20 to 29. The defendants had allegedly left South Africa in 1976 and received military training in Angola, returning to South Africa between November 1979 and February 1980 with the intention of conducting armed struggle and committing acts of sabotage. They were accused of attacking the Soekmekaar police station using three hand grenades and firing 56 shots with an AK47 rifle. They were alleged to have made plans for numerous other attacks, including that on the Volkskas bank January 25, during which two hostages and three guerrillas were killed.

The defendants were found guilty of high treason. Three were sentenced to death. Two received twenty-year sentences, two fifteen years and two ten years.

2. Bhekizitha Nqubelani appeared in Cape Town Supreme Court in March, charged with violating the Terrorism Act and with attempted murder. He had allegedly received military training in Botswana and Angola and returned with explosives, arms and ammunition to commit sabotage and recruit others for military training in foreign countries. He

---

*New York Times,* July 4, 1982, p. 4.

was also charged with having planted a bomb, which did not explode, in the Cape Town Supreme Court.

Nqubelani was found guilty on four counts and given sentences which totalled twenty-five years, five years of which were to be served concurrently. The judge noted that he did not impose the death penalty, but only because Nqubelani was motivated by idealism and prompted by frustration.

3. A group of nine Africans, including one 16-year-old and four 18-year-olds, were charged with having been recruited and having recruited others to receive military training outside of South Africa in order to return and overthrow the government with violence.

One defendant was freed. Two received seven-year sentences and the others were given five-year sentences.

4. Dr. Renfrew Christie, a research fellow at the University of Cape Town, was charged with conveying information to the International University Exchange Fund and the ANC about South African atomic energy production. He was found guilty and received a thirty-year sentence.

5. In a less dramatic trial that was not a "major" trial but was indicative of South African security efforts, two young men, one the president of the Congress of South African Students and the other a student at the University of the North, were charged with promoting the aims of ANC by distributing pamphlets. They were also accused of establishing youth clubs to promote unrest. The defendants were charged under the Terrorism Act, the Internal Security Act and the Unlawful Organization Act.

The defendants were found guilty and each sentenced to eight years in prison.

**Political Violence**

There is more politically motivated violence in South Africa than is generally assumed. Here are some examples:

1. On January 4 three men attacked the Soekmekaar police station in Lebowa with AK47 rifles and hand grenades. No damage was caused. One policeman was slightly injured (See Security Trials, 1, above).

2. On January 8 a man was killed at Duiwelskloof, and an arms cache was found nearby.

3. Also on January 8 petrol bombs were thrown in Port Elizabeth at homes of Ford workers who had returned to work against the decision of other workers.

4. On January 15 an attempt was made to blow up a Port Elizabeth supermarket owned by a political dissident.

5. On January 22 a man and two children were injured in a bomb explosion in Atteridgeville, Pretoria.

6. On January 25 three guerrillas took over the Volkskas bank and twenty-five hostages in Silverton, Pretoria. Political demands, not disclosed

by the police, were made. In a police shootout, the three guerrillas and two hostages were killed. Nine hostages and two policemen were seriously wounded.

7. In January an arsenal of rocket launchers, guns, ammunition and explosives, plus quantities of ANC pamphlets, were found near Springs. Other caches of arms were found in northern Natal, northern Zululand, near Durban, Western Transvaal and Pondoland.

8. In March three people were killed and two seriously injured by a hand grenade in northern Transkei.

9. Also in March two guerrillas were arrested in Mondlo Township in northern Natal, and some arms and ammunition were found.

10. In Bophuthatswana in March three guerrillas clashed with security forces. One escaped and two were killed. A large arms cache was found.

11. On April 4 eleven guerrillas attacked Booysens police station in Johannesburg, using hand grenades, RPG-7 rocket launchers and AK47 rifles.

12. On June 1 there were bombings at SASOL I, one of the plants making gasoline from coal. Damages were estimated at about $8,000,000. ANC and the South African Communist Party claimed responsibility.

13. On June 2 three bombs were found and defused at the recruiting offices of the South African Coal, Oil and Gas Corporation in Springs.

14. In July there were fires destroying the Yeoville telephone exchange and a plastics factory in Edenvale for which the ANC claimed responsibility. Authorities listed other causes.

15. An expelled former ANC official working for the Transkei government was killed. ANC was blamed for the death.

16. There were a number of incidents in August, including a bomb found near Emmerentia Dam, a bomb exploding near Heatonville injuring two children, two men killed by a hand grenade in Sandton, and a security man shot at with an AK 47 rifle in Sabantu Village.

17. On October 15 the main Soweto–Johannesburg railroad line was blown up at Dube causing a four-hour disruption of traffic. ANC pamphlets were found at the scene.

18. On October 29 two hand grenades exploded in a government office in Soweto injuring two persons and causing extensive damage to the building.

19. On October 30 the house of the Transkei consul in Port Elizabeth was damaged by a bomb. There were no injuries.

20. On November 21 there was a shootout between a man in a house in Soweto and the police. The man was killed by the explosion of a grenade in his hand.

21. There were at least two bombings for which a rightwing organization stated its responsibility and many threats by rightwing white organizations in 1980. There were no arrests for rightwing political violence. (There were two convictions in 1981.)

Resistance is very much alive in South Africa and is being seen daily across the country, sometimes in small ways, sometimes dramatically. In an obviously incomplete list the *Los Angeles Times* reports "37 incidents of sabotage and terrorism" in South Africa in the first eight months of 1981. South African police have reported 300 incidents in 1980–81. More often than otherwise, the resistance is nonviolent, but that is never considered newsworthy. It is said that much violent resistance never gets into the newspapers either, because it is no longer news. It is also alleged that government reulations keep some sabotage from getting reported. This chapter, laden with resistance action, is all based on the public record, but most of this resistance appeared only in the local papers. Legal restrictions on the press inhibit full reporting (see Chapter 2, Enforcement). The South African Broadcasting Corporation is controlled by the South African government, so radio and TV news is handled "safely." Hence, only the most highly dramatic incidents are reported in the United States.

Tourism is big business in South Africa. It is encouraged to boost foreign exchange and as a propaganda tool. Most tourists will stay in a five-star hotel (and be impressed by an African guest or two), go shopping, visit the game parks, go down into a mine and wonder what all the controversy is about. Many tourists have written their home newspaper to say they've been in South Africa and everything is peaceful. That is the kind of reporting which the supporters of apartheid promote. But South Africa simmers with resistance. Any day can bring a new boiling over—a Defiance Campaign, a Soweto rebellion, a Sharpeville Massacre.

# CHAPTER 5

# *South Africa's Geopolitical Context*

Countries are affected by events outside their borders as well as by those within them. This is true even when, as in the case of South Africa, there are vigorous elements pressing for the country's isolation from the rest of the world. From the outside, economic, sports and arts boycotts are organized as campaigns against apartheid. South African representatives often find their participation challenged at international conferences. The United Nations approved a voluntary arms embargo against South Africa in 1963 after the Sharpeville Massacre and a mandatory arms embargo in November 1977 after the Soweto uprising. In 1981 a campaign for economic sanctions was renewed within the General Assembly.

Forces from within also push the South African government toward isolation. Many white South Africans believe that apartheid is an internal matter and that the system is either satisfactory and should be of no concern to the rest of the world, or it is a problem which can best be solved if South Africa is left alone to solve it.

In spite of these pressures toward isolation, South Africa is very much part of the world; it is a resource-rich country with highly developed industrial and commercial sectors that are intricately linked with the western economy. The United States and other countries consider South Africa economically and strategically important. Further, as the last white-ruled country in Africa and the only country in the world where racial privilege is enforced by law, South Africa necessarily attracts international attention.

## Regional Influences

South Africa is connected by history, geography and economic interests to the other nine states of southern Africa—Angola, Botswana, Lesotho, Malawi, Mozambique, Namibia, Swaziland, Zambia, Zimbabwe. The slave trade and the discovery of gold brought Europeans to the coast of Angola, and Arabs and Europeans to the coast of Mozambique. It was from the Cape of Good Hope in the seventeenth century that the settlers from Europe began the push north and east into the interior of South Africa. Cecil Rhodes, from England, provided the intiative for opening the interior beyond South Africa in order to develop mines and extend the British Empire, and the majority of early settlers were British. As a result of Rhodes's efforts the center of southern Africa became a British colonial territory during the latter half of the nineteenth century. Later, Afrikaner farmers, who looked to South Africa instead of Europe as the motherland, eventually became an economic and political power base within the areas now comprising Zambia and Zimbabwe, and to a lesser extent Botswana.

Communication flowed north and south as roads and railroads were built from the interior to South Africa and its ports. Other railroads were built to connect Zambia, Zimbabwe and Malawi to ports in Mozambique, and another through Angola, with the result that southern Africa was further developed as an interdependent economic unit. The only northern commercial routes out of the area, other than by air, are an all-weather highway

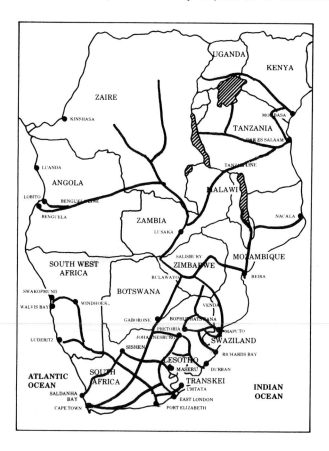

MAJOR RAILWAYS OF SOUTHERN AFRICA

From *Backgrounder,* September 1981, courtesy of the South Africa Department of Foreign Affairs and Information, Pretoria.

built with U.S. assistance and a railroad from Zambia to Dar es Salaam built by the People's Republic of China after Zambia's independence. The use of that railroad has been severely curtailed because of difficulties with the Dar es Salaam port, having become a target for bombing by Rhodesia during the Zimbabwe struggles for independence and because of its limited capabilities.

Botswana (then Bechuanaland), Lesotho (then Basutoland) and Swaziland were British protectorates. As South Africa's racial policies developed, British and South African expectations that these countries would be joined to South Africa were dropped, and they became independent states in the late 1960s. They remain, however, closely connected to the South African economy and are part of the Southern Africa Customs Union in which South Africa takes a leading role.

Malawi is the only African country currently maintaining full diplomatic relations with South Africa. South Africa has given economic assistance to Malawi, including a major grant to relocate the capital city. Men from Malawi work in South Africa's mines, although in much smaller numbers than in former years, and South Africa is Malawi's main trading partner.

Zambia is also tied economically to South Africa, buying food and some manufactured products and exporting some copper through South African ports. An alternative rail route for Zambia's exports through Angola remains unreliable because of guerrilla warfare waged against the Angolan government.

Zimbabwe has been closely connected to South Africa in many ways since its Rhodesian beginning. This relationship was intensified during the days of the Unilateral Declaration of Independence (UDI) as South Africa filled many of the economic gaps created by the UN boycott against the government of Ian Smith. Many whites now in Zimbabwe originally came from South Africa, and many of Zimbabwe's present black leaders received part of their education there. Whites travel extensively between the two countries for vacations and on business, and South African individuals and companies remain the largest outside investors in Zimbabwe.

Like Zimbabwe, Mozambique has been closely tied into the South African economy. Mozambican men working in the mines of South Africa continue to be a key source of foreign exchange for their country. Cabora Bassa, a large hydroelectric plant in the center of Mozambique, supplies electricity almost exclusively for South Africa. South African personnel operate ports in Mozambique and are key to the operation of the railroad.

Angola has been the country of southern Africa least related to South Africa. Since 1975, the guerrilla fight to free Namibia from South African control has created a virtual state of war between South Africa and Angola. SWAPO, the main Namibian liberation movement, operates from bases in Angola, and South Africa stages both ground and air attacks in Angola in retaliation. Furthermore, South Africa supports UNITA (National Union for the Total Independence of Angola), composed of dissident Angolan forces, in its guerrilla warfare against the Angolan government, exacerbating tensions between the countries.

The mineral-rich, sparsely populated country of Namibia is closely tied to South Africa economically as well as politically. Most of the country's food and consumer goods are imported from South Africa. The two harbors, Luderitz and Walvis Bay, are operated by South African Railways. All of its diamonds (Namibia is the second largest producer after South Africa) are produced for export by a subsidiary of De Beers, Consolidated Mines of South Africa, Ltd. The rich but now dangerously depleted fishing grounds off the Namibian coast and the fish processing plants there were once second only to mining in economic importance.

South Africa has allowed other countries to exploit the many mineral resources of Namibia. The Tsumeb mine in northern Namibia is one of the larger base metal mines in the world. It is jointly controlled by an American company, AMAX, and the Newmont Mining Corporation, which is owned by Anglo American, a British/South African company. Namibia is believed to be the third largest source of uranium in the world and has the world's largest uranium oxide pit. The Rossing uranium mine at Swakopmund near Walvis Bay is particularly controversial. First, it was opened in 1976 in violation of the 1970 Security Council Resolution 283, which called on all states to take a series of measures designed to end any trade or commercial dealings and investments by their nationals in Namibia. Second, the uranium could contribute to South Africa's development of nuclear weapons.

Namibia is tied not only to South Africa, but to other countries in southern Africa and to the world because of its history as a Mandated Territory. Namibia is especially linked to its neighbors, Angola and Zambia, both of which have provided shelter to refugees and support to SWAPO and as a result have suffered attacks by the South African Defense Forces. Lusaka, Zambia is the home of the UN Institute for Namibia, where future administrators and leaders of Namibia are trained. Botswana has also accepted Namibian refugees.

No matter how much they detest apartheid, the other states of southern Africa have found it impossible to sever all relationships with South Africa because of the historical alignment of trade and transportation. The eight majority-ruled countries of southern Africa, together with Tanzania, have established an organization (Southern African Development Coordination Conference, SADCC) and a process, including periodic conferences, to seek ways to improve agricultural production, communications and trade, thus increasing their collective self-sufficiency and decreasing their dependence on South Africa. The SADCC should also strengthen the power of neighboring countries in negotiations with South Africa. The SADCC agreement was signed April 1, 1980 in Lusaka.

The economic dependence on South Africa of the states of the region is an important element in her prosperity. This dependence also lessens South Africa's isolation from the rest of the world. The South African government has proposed to use these interrelationships as a basis for a "constellation" of southern African states, including the "independent" homelands as participants. For obvious political reasons no such structured common market approach to southern Africa is possible as long as minority rule continues in South Africa. An economically strong southern Africa confederation may develop after majority rule is achieved.

## The Independence Movement

From the 1950s to the 1970s, majority rule progressed from the northern countries southward. White South Africans considered themselves insulated by the Portugese colonies of Mozambique and Angola, by white-dominated Southern Rhodesia, by an economically dependent Botswana and politically controlled Namibia. When Mozambique and Angola gained freedom from Portugal in 1975, and Zimbabwe gained majority rule in 1980, the situation was radically altered. Still, a political transformation in South Africa seems remote.

Why have the forces which moved the other African states to majority rule not yet moved South Africa? The other African countries that gained majority governments in this period had different histories of colonization from that of South Africa. From the formation of the Union of South Africa in 1910, white minority rule in South Africa has not been a traditional colonialism. Most white South Africans do not feel linked to a European homeland to which they may return, nor does any European or other national group have even nominal political authority in South Africa. In all the other situations, there was an external power to grant independence, however reluctantly and belatedly. In South Africa majority rule will have to be gained in the political context of the country itself.

Part of that context is the market for labor. Although there were some whites in both Zimbabwe and Mozambique who saw "one person–one vote" as a threat to their jobs, the fear of black competition on the labor market is far greater and more real in South Africa than it was in any other African country.

Nonetheless, the same forces which brought increasingly irresistable pressure against colonialism in Africa continue to build up against the rule by whites in South Africa. There are forces such as those created by Pan Africanism, the Organization of African Unity, the independence and increasing power of Third World countries around the world, and the development of a Third World majority in the United Nations "one nation–one vote" General Assembly.

As colonialism was interwoven with racism, so anticolonialism is related to antiracism. Racism is central to the problem of South Africa. Efforts to deal with racism in other parts of the world, notably the United States, have had an impact on South Africa. Black consciousness in the United States and in South Africa have had parallel and independent developments, but the movement in the 1960s in the U.S. had a definite impact on the South African movement. Conversely, the leaders of independent African countries have inspired black civil rights leaders in the U.S.

Black and white South Africans hold different views on the result of the elimination of colonialism from the continent and the heightened world awareness of racism. Both recognize an impact on their own country. Blacks see that most of the governments of their neighboring states grant dignity to all their citizens, black and white, seek to equalize economic opportunity as well as political status, and overcome both the spirit and effects of racism. Blacks also see majority governments as supportive of their own struggle for liberation. Generally, white South Africans fear the momentum of change as the movement for independence presses south. They believe that African rule has usually been corrupt, destructive of national economies and subject to coups. They believe there are few free elections. Many cite Idi Amin of Uganda as a typical African leader. This image is what they expect for South Africa under a one person–one vote structure (and, they usually add, one election). Their view of independent Africa is maintained and reinforced by a pattern of limited access to information about events in other parts of Africa and by the government's official version of events. Some white South Africans, however, also admit the inevitability of majority rule and seek ways to accommodate themselves to this change. A major Afrikaans newspaper, reporting on the election of Mugabe in Zimbabwe, exhorted white South Africa to acknowledge its relevance to their own country, saying, "We must learn that to try to preserve everything is to lose everything."

## Anticommunism

Anticommunism fuels much of white South Africa's fear of and resistance to change. An anticommunist hysteria is orchestrated and promoted by some leaders in order to strengthen commitment to the present system. In this view, communists get all the credit or blame for the resistance to apartheid. Paradoxically, white anticommunism prompts more black interest in communism than results from any particular communist effectiveness. An illegal Communist Party does exist underground in South Africa, and a few members have been prosecuted.

Much of South Africa's concern centers around communist support for liberation movements. The Soviet Union supports the African National Congress (ANC), one of two major liberation movements in South Africa, while the other, the Pan Africanist Congress (PAC), receives some support from China. South African leaders are far more concerned about the Soviet Union than about China. The Chinese have maintained a low profile in Africa, giving some economic assistance and military training in Tanzania, in addition to some aid to liberation groups. The largest aid project supported by the Chinese is the railroad that links Zambia to the Tanzania port of Dar es Salaam, a project turned down by the World Bank and other Western donors as not economically feasible.

SWAPO receives strong support from Moscow, and South Africa continually raises that issue. Preoccupation with communism obscures the reality that liberation movements are, first of all, nationalist. They are also pragmatic and will accept help from wherever it comes. Communist countries have helped most of the liberation movements of southern Africa, which have often sought support from western nations and been turned down. In spite of these relationships, once free, the new nations act in their own perceived interests. Both the United States and the Soviet Union have often been disappointed with the consistent nonalignment of independent southern African states. The liberation movements have never been willing to trade one colonial overlord for another.

Zimbabwe is an excellent example of this. Robert Mugabe, now Prime Minister, was seen by most whites in South Africa and Southern Rhodesia as the epitome of communist evil when he led his guerrilla forces against Rhodesia. These whites expected him, if he won power, to establish a communist government which would be ruthless in dealing with white leaders and in suppression of civil rights and economic free enterprise. It was expected that representatives of communist governments would be welcomed with open arms. Yet, in office, Mugabe has led a reconciling, nonracist government. The first embassy established in Zimbabwe was that of the United States, on the first day of independence. There were many months of negotiations before the embassy of the Soviet Union was accepted.

The U.S. is also preoccupied with anticommunism. Therefore, both South Africa and the U.S. have focused on the presence of troops in Africa from communist countries, while ignoring those from other parts of the world. Black Africans express concern about the role of foreign troops from whatever country. They ask: To whom are the troops responsible? At whose invitation are they present? Whose interests do they protect? AFSC visitors to the frontline states in 1977 were frequently asked why questions were raised only about Cuban troops and not about the French. Until 1980, when they withdrew from Chad, the French had the largest number of foreign troops in Africa.

Not only is anticommunism used by South Africa to solidify internal resistance to change, it is also exploited to gain support for the current South African regime from the United States and other Western nations. South Africa's minerals and the sea route around the Cape are seen by some as of strategic interest to the "free world." Significant numbers of white South Africans believe, or hope, that if a violent showdown comes, the United States can be relied on for support to "defeat communism." Western support for apartheid is justified by the East/West conflict.

Fear of communist attack from outside or within gives justification for a military machine that is stronger than those of any combination of the surrounding states. There is a rigidly enforced military conscription law for every able-bodied white male. White males remain liable for compulsory military duty to age 65. Other races are in the armed forces on a volunteer basis. All races may now receive training in the use of arms and white women are actively recruited into the military. Emergency legislation and planning provide total mobilization of people and industry, including U.S.-owned industry. The armed forces are used regularly as part of the internal security operation in cases of civilian demonstrations and disturbances.

There is a high probability that South Africa has produced a nuclear weapon. In any event, its capability to do so adds a new dimension to its destructive potential. Nuclear weapons are useless for internal warfare but pose a threat to countries such as Nigeria, which has been a leader against apartheid. In the world context, nuclear weapons in the hands of South Africa would represent one more dangerous step in nuclear proliferation. Moreover, South Africa has not signed the UN nonproliferation treaty.

## Soviet Policy

Because of the fear of Soviet communism expressed by South Africa, it is important to assess Soviet policies in the area, even though these are difficult to know with any certainty. As with most countries, Soviet foreign policy is a mix of ideological and pragmatic elements. Ideologically, the Soviets appear to operate on two bases. First, there is a commitment to socialism and, when possible, to its extension to other societies, which leads to the support of liberation movements in a number of places. Second, the superpower conflict gives rise to anti-Americanism, an ideological stance which has its mirror image in U.S. anti-Sovietism. Pragmatically, the Soviet Union seeks to support its perceived national interest around the world, befriending potential allies, especially in economically or militarily strategic locations, and trying to assure that U.S. influence is limited and undermined.

One way to understand Soviet policies in southern Africa is to look at the record of Soviet involvements in Africa over recent decades. These policies have seldom been successful in establishing influence. Starting with Ghana in 1966, the Soviet Union has been invited *out* of as many countries as those with which it has been able to establish long-term relationships. In 1974, Egypt, Sudan and Somalia were three of the largest recipients of Soviet military aid to Africa, but in all three Soviet forces were subsequently expelled (Sudan in 1971, Egypt in 1975 and Somalia in 1978). Soviet involvement in Guinea ended in 1979. In recent years, the U.S.S.R. has concentrated its attentions in Africa on four countries—Algeria, Libya, Angola and Ethiopia. Involvement in three of these has much to do with the superpower conflict around the Middle East and Persian Gulf area.

In no case has the Soviet Union committed large numbers of its own troops to African countries. In 1980, approximately seven thousand Soviet and Warsaw Pact military personnel were serving in Africa as military advisers and technicians, primarily in the four countries named above. This number has remained relatively stable over the past ten years, though the countries in which they are placed have changed.* Cuban troops and advisors, totalling approximately thirty-seven thousand and three thousand respectively, have greatly increased communist involvement.** Soviet relations with Algeria and Libya have been stable and durable, but the majority of these military and technical personnel are located in Angola and Ethiopia. There Soviet and allied presence followed a request by the local ruling authorities when they were involved in conflict with neighboring countries. This aid was requested and granted after the same request was turned down by the West. In Angola heavy Soviet and Cuban involvement occurred after October 1975 when South African and Zairean troops invaded to try to prevent the Soviet supported MPLA (Popular Movement for the Liberation of Angola) from gaining control of the newly independent country. Soviet and Cuban involvement in Ethiopia occurred in response to the Somalian invasion of the Ogaden region and to the attempts of the Eritreans to establish an independent state.

In many instances, the Soviet Union and the People's Republic of China have supported opposing liberation groups, an extension of their own ideological and strategic conflict. This was true in Southern Rhodesia and remains so in Angola. Soviet interests in Africa seem to include its competition with China as well as with the United States.

From 1973 to 1978 external arms transfers to Africa increased tenfold, making Africa the largest arms market in the Third World after the Middle East. All suppliers' sales increased dramatically, especially those of the

---

*International Institute for Strategic Studies, *This Military Balance 1972–73,* London, 1972, p. 2.

**Daniel Volman, *A Continent Besieged: Foreign Military Activities in Africa Since 1975,* Institute for Policy Studies Report, Washington, D.C., 1980, p. 4.

three largest—the Soviet Union, France and the United States. Current Soviet arms involvements in Africa far exceed those of either France or the U.S.; the U.S.S.R. supplies about 50% of all arms to Africa, France about 25% and the U.S. about 13%.* South Africa spends about two billion dollars per year on defense and is able to manufacture most of the arms it uses.

While it is obvious that the Soviet Union and its allies are involved in the African continent, it is also clear that this involvement has changed recently in response to changing conditions within the African countries themselves. The Soviet Union has not been able to "call the shots" or achieve the stable relationships it may have wished for. In no case has the Soviet Union tried to cut off the access of the West to the continent's mineral resources or to seize Western economic interests. U.S. firms continue to operate in both Algeria and Angola, for example. These states, despite reliance on the U.S.S.R., invite and encourage U.S. business interests and investments. In fact, trade between the Soviet Union and South Africa, though small, has been increasing and frequent reports tell of Soviet and South African collaboration in the sale of gold, diamonds and platinum on the world market.

There is little evidence to support claims that the Soviet Union is involved in a campaign to establish itself strongly throughout Africa. This may be partly the result of its unwillingness or inability to supply the economic assistance that would be required to sustain such a campaign. In any event, Soviet experience and overextension in Afghanistan would seem likely to cool ambitions for political and military expansion to control any African countries. The U.S.S.R. is aware of the attitudes of the African nations themselves, which welcome no overlord even as they accept economic and military aid from whatever source. The context of circumstances which have shaped Soviet policy in Africa seem unlikely to change in the foreseeable future. There is little reason to expect that the Soviet Union will attempt any major alterations in its relations with the countries of Africa.

Insofar as South Africa is concerned, any threat to the present regime arises from internal dissent rather than from armed invasion by the U.S.S.R. or its allies. In South Africa, as has been true in so many other times and places, external "threat" is a handy justification for tightening internal control.

## North/South Division

In addition to the East/West division, the North/South world division also affects South Africa. The latter division arises not from political

---

*Daniel Volman, *A Continent Besieged,* p. 4.

systems but from differences in the level of industrialization. The richer nations are concentrated in the northern hemisphere and the poorer nations in the southern hemisphere. Within the United Nations, there are increasing demands and pressures from the nonaligned nations for the North to accept greater responsibility for its role in the poverty of the South. White South Africa identifies, in many ways, with the North. Its cultural heritage, level of personal income and increasingly industrialized economic base are most consistent with the North; but what is not consistent is its minority racial status.

So in terms of affluence, white South Africa identifies with the North, and in terms of economic and political organization with the West. Black South Africa shares neither identification. Its ties are clearly to its own continent and, therefore, to the South. Many black South Africans and the two major liberation movements reject the economic inequality and domination which they see resulting from the South African version of state managed capitalism. They also reject Soviet socialism as their model, as does the growing group of nonaligned nations. They seek an alternative organizational form of socialism which grows out of their own cultural context and which results in a more equitable distribution of resources and democratic political arrangements. To make the point that they seek these new ways, the countries of east and southern Africa often describe their political and economic systems and goals as African socialism.

## U.S. Policy

After decades of neglect and following World War II, the United States began to pay serious attention to the continent of Africa. The uncertainty among policy framers of the relative importance to the U.S. of various regions of the continent (North, Arab; tropical, black African; southern Africa, predominantly colonial and white dominated in 1945) has persisted to this day. Colonialism has almost disappeared. The African caucus, with other Third World support, carries considerable influence at the United Nations. Great mineral wealth has been exploited in the south, largely by white regimes and oil has been found in North and West Africa. Thus, the continent has greatly changed since 1945. For decades changing administrations in Washington have followed a relatively consistent policy: keep on good terms with all African nations, but cater especially to those whose raw materials, markets, investment opportunities, and strategic location suggest they are of the most importance to our national interest. U.S. officials were disconcerted when they found that a neutral or balanced posture among competing interests was almost impossible.

Black nations, newly liberated from European colonialism, could not ignore the remaining minority regimes or their racial policies. They sought sympathy and support from the U.S., as a major power whose history and rhetoric suggested understanding of their needs. On many occasions, however, they felt rebuffed as they saw the U.S. lean toward European allies in NATO or toward conservative white minority regimes, presumably for strategic reasons. South Africa played up affinities with the U.S. and encouraged a growing economic relationship, with considerable success.

U.S. African policy over several administrations has been fashioned to satisfy various disparate interests on the home front and to support a foreign policy designed to check the Soviet Union. Access to vital minerals was set as a priority alongside protection of the sea route around the Cape. Only recently has the growing importance of trade with black Africa (for example oil from Nigeria and chrome from Zimbabwe), coupled with some increasing sensitivity to human rights issues abroad influenced by U.S. civil rights efforts, brought about an apparent modification in the United States' cooperation with South Africa.

The previous and the present administrations both carried out policies that reveal the dilemmas implicit in the conflicting claims of various American interests. Experience, especially under Carter, also suggests that there are steps a government can take that may have some desired impact on a foreign state's policies. South Africa consciously claimed "reforms" in its race relations, partially to reassure the U.S.

Chief spokespersons of the Carter Administration were Andrew Young and Donald McHenry at the UN and Richard Moose in Washington. If not the architects, they were seen as major figures in policy framing and were much resented by the South African government. The Reagan election victory in 1980 brought official satisfaction and also private celebrations in South Africa. A new and friendlier face would be looking at their problems from Washington, D.C.

How different have the new policies of the Reagan Administration proved thus far? In addition to those of President Reagan and Secretary of State Haig, policy statements have also been made by Chester Crocker, Assistant Secretary of State for Africa and by Jeane Kirkpatrick, U.S. Ambassador to the UN.

Comparing broad statements of policy by Moose and Crocker, one finds little difference and much agreement on substance. Emphases do differ, however. Moose summarizes U.S. policy on South Africa as follows:

1. "to preserve our national consensus on foreign policy goals relating to human rights and human dignity."

2. to assure "long-term access to strategic minerals in South Africa and surrounding countries. . . ."

3. to foreclose "opportunities for expanded Soviet influence that come with protracted violent conflict. (Testimony before House of Representatives, Committee on Foreign Affairs, Subcommittee on Africa, 30 April 1980)

Before joining the State Department, Chester Crocker was director of African Studies at the Center for Strategic and International Studies at Georgetown University. In that capacity he made detailed policy statements about South Africa. (See *Freedom at Issue*, November/December 1980, reprinted in *Africa Report*, January/February 1981 and his testimony before the Subcommittee on Africa of the House of Representatives 10 June 1980). Crocker's views on South Africa are more in harmony with liberal opinion than his own statements about Carter and human rights or the Reagan attitude in general seem to reflect.

Crocker sees southern Africa as a unit and the importance of Zimbabwe, as well as South Africa, to that unit. He has been outspoken on more aid to Zimbabwe. He also says that African states cannot be easily distinguished as "hostiles" and "friendlies" using Marxist rhetoric as the litmus test. As to attacks on surrounding countries by South Africa, Crocker states, "We must be prepared to help governments to retain primacy over guerrillas on their own territory and to defend their soveriegnty if South Africa overplays its military superiority." On Namibia, Crocker says, "The United States and its allies have nothing to gain from backing a South African client government in circumstances that assure a continuation of internationalized warfare." He understands that "in political terms, South Africa is not embraceable without our incurring massive diplomatic damage and risking severe domestic polarization." Crocker frequently mentions the limitation on foreign policy imposed by public opinion. In this respect he observes that "even if Washington publicly promised military support of Pretoria to meet its internal challenges, there is no way that any U.S. administration could meet this commitment."

On the other hand, Crocker stresses the lack of U.S. coercive power to change South African policies. He is against sanctions, boycotts and divestment. He does not want to emphasize ultimate goals such as "end apartheid" or "one person–one vote." He thinks the U.S. should urge continuous movement by South Africa and encourage, perhaps reward, good steps, while remaining critical of wrong moves or pretenses of change. He and President Reagan seem to agree that the U.S. should be helpful to South Africa as long as "sincere and honest effort" is being made toward ending racism. This leaves much room for argument about every phase of actual or claimed change. As for South Africa, Prime Minister Botha's assertion is that he has made nothing but sincere and honest efforts to end racism ever since getting into office.

Crocker's speech in Honolulu in 1981 about not supporting either blacks or whites in South Africa seems a step backward, even for the Reagan administration. There is surely some more positive role for the U.S. than "hands off." Although we do not agree with many of the steps taken and do regret many steps not taken by the Carter Administration, the AFSC sees as accurate the U.S. policy dilemma posed by Richard Moose in his testimony before the Subcommittee on Africa. "How," he asked, "can we maintain credibility with all parties in a segregated society? . . . How can we communicate approval of individual steps while still calling for other steps not yet taken?"

Placing a concern for human dignity ahead of assuring access to minerals was intentional on the part of Moose, even though he believed the issues were too interrelated to separate. He believed that the advancement of human rights was the best guarantee for keeping minerals available and avoiding Russian involvement. The main thrust of the Carter policy on South Africa was to encourage peaceful, rapid change. The objective was good but the implementation weak. The Carter Administration believed that its ability to influence events in South Africa was severely limited. Such a belief, we think, is self-fulfilling.

The specific Reagan Administration policy on South Africa is taking shape, after some confusing early statements. The specifics are less clear than the broad outline which appears similar to that of the Carter Administration, suggesting a high degree of continuity. The emphases are patently different, however.

Reagan makes it clear that his administration is trying a friendlier posture towards South Africa. This is shown in words (or lack of them) and deeds in Washington, New York and Pretoria. There is less condemnation of apartheid, more military consultation and economic cooperation. The "tilt" perceived by African diplomats and other observers takes many forms. Actions are taken by South African officials without fear of criticism by the U.S., for example: aborting the Geneva conference on Namibia, military incursions into neighboring African States, especially Angola, and tougher domestic policies. South African officials are being welcomed to Washington as they have not been for years. The Reagan Administration has lifted the ban on the sale of antihijacking gear to South African police and military and relaxed other restrictions on sales. A license was issued for the export of a large Univac computer to a subsidiary of the South African government's parastatal corporation for arms production.

The key issue in 1982–83 is independence for the people of Namibia. Carter pressed hard through negotiations directly and in concert with other Western partners, together with active participation in UN efforts against discrimination, but Reagan appears to be working more on his own. He is using a carrot in seeking what may be the same goal. It is not clear that alternative or fallback tactics are on the drawing board. Observers are not sanguine that this approach alone will bring the desired result. The independent British periodical *The Economist* editorialized in September 1981:

> The Americans have made a mistake in assuming that the South African government's response to gentle handling would be to show a corresponding restraint. Instead of seizing Reagan's

outstretched hand, Mr. Botha has to all intents and purposes bit-
ten it. In recent weeks, besides the deep military thrust into
Angola, there have been smaller but significant South African incursions into other black-ruled neighbor states, including, for the
first time, into Lesotho.

Much rests on the approach to the Namibia negotiations. If successful—and we hope it will be—the strategy will be applauded. If it fails,
this administration may enter a drawn-out military morass and/or participate in prolonged fruitless discussions.

The U.S. action in vetoing a Security Council denunciation of the South
African military foray into Angola illustrates the problem of securing South
African cooperation. As *The Economist* again exclaimed:

> The Soviet and South African governments were delighted by
> the American use of the veto in the UN Security Council (August
> 31, 1981) against a formal condemnation of the South African
> armed forces' incursion into Angola. Although the motion was
> not well-worded, this veto has infuriated many of the three-
> quarters of the people of the world who are humiliated by white
> South Africa's racial policies. It has strengthened Mr. Pieter
> Botha and his South African cabinet in the belief that they can
> count on American protection. It has obliged the friends and
> allies of the U.S. to stand apart from it. These are heavy prices to
> pay. They include some practical prices in the Third World. An
> internationally acceptable settlement in Namibia—one that might
> have got the Cubans out of Angola—will now be harder to get.
> Next time America needs the help of a third party, as it needed
> Algeria's to get its hostages out of Iran, some of the necessary
> thrust may be found no longer to exist. Support at the UN for
> resolutions condemning Russia—as for instance, after the inva-
> sion of Afghanistan—may not be so forthcoming in the future.
> America has forfeited, at least for a time, some influence in
> guiding economic development in black Africa and in moderating
> its extremists. By spitting into the wind of change it has encour-
> aged the Qaddafis of the continent. . . .

If this dismal prophecy materializes, what fallback position do Reagan
and Crocker have? Not only have they alienated much of the world that
finds apartheid totally reprehensible, they have given South Africa much of
what it has sought—U.S. support—without gaining significant concessions.
Independence for Namibia still seems far away. Domestic South African
policies appear tougher than a few months ago. Have military, strategic,
and commercial considerations, reinforced by a knee-jerk reaction to the
U.S.S.R., eroded America's commitment to human rights? It was this commitment that earned U.S. influence in Africa and supported the liberation
of Namibia and the end of apartheid. Too high a price is being paid for a
doubtful tactic.

However the policy is articulated and implemented, it is clear that an informed, vocal American public opinion is more important than ever for keeping the U.S. from supporting oppressive regimes such as South Africa's, especially when it appears that the support arises from ill-conceived strategic and economic concerns that discount the human factor.

# CHAPTER 6

# *International Pressure on Apartheid*

Because of its policy of apartheid, South Africa is facing increasing criticism from other countries. This criticism and the effort to end apartheid come from a variety of international organizations. In some instances international corporations have also become a force from outside of South Africa involved in the political issues of apartheid. In this chapter international pressures on apartheid will be examined and some assessment made of the effectiveness of that pressure.

Many international organizations such as sporting bodies, labor groups and religious organizations have been critical of apartheid. These organizations have passed resolutions, banned South African representatives from attendance at meetings, contributed to the support of liberation movements, helped refugees from South Africa and Namibia, boycotted South African products, divested themselves of stock in corporations doing business in South Africa and found many other ways to express their displeasure. Although others have done much, the Organization of African Unity and the United Nations have maintained the most active and most continuous protest against the South African policies.

## Organization of African Unity

In 1963 at Addis Ababa the Organization of African Unity was formed. The OAU is a voluntary association of African states which seeks to address continental issues. While the countries are diverse economically and politically, they have always been in agreement in their opposition to apartheid. The OAU has spearheaded international action related to South Africa's minority government. At the time of its inception, many African states were still colonized, and six of its original fifteen resolutions affirmed the OAU's support for liberation movements in the Portuguese colonies, Southern Rhodesia, Namibia and South Africa. Resolution 12 of the charter document established a "Special Fund to be raised by voluntary contribution of Member States . . . to supply the necessary practical and financial aid to the various African national liberation movements."

The OAU adopted a nine-point policy specifically aimed at South Africa to "put an end to the South African Government's criminal policy of apartheid and wipe out racial discrimination in all its forms.'' The points centered around sanctions, diplomatic isolation, support for efforts within the United Nations and appeals to all governments to support the struggle against the South African regime. The final point expressed "appreciation for the efforts of the Federal Government of the United States of America to put an end to these intolerable malpractices which are likely seriously to deteriorate relations between the African peoples and governments on the one hand and the people and government of the United States on the other.'' In this era there was hope and expectation that the United States would use its moral and economic power to help bring majority rule in South Africa.

In 1969, at a meeting in Lusaka, Zambia, fourteen states from east and central Africa agreed upon a manifesto which said:

> We have always preferred and we still prefer to achieve liberation without physical violence. We would prefer to negotiate rather than to destroy, to talk rather than kill. We do not advocate violence; we advocate an end to violence against human dignity which is now being perpetrated by the oppressors of Africa. If peaceful progress to emancipation were possible, or if changed circumstances were to make it possible in the future, we would urge our brothers in the resistance movements to use peaceful methods of struggle *even at the cost of some compromise on the timing of change* (emphasis added).

This manifesto was subsequently adopted in September 1969 by the Organization of African Unity and, later, by the General Assembly of the United Nations.

In spite of their reluctance, liberation movements in Africa have all utilized armed force, as well as negotiations, to make the status quo untenable and to concentrate international pressure to support them. In 1972 at its meeting at Rabat, Morocco, the OAU noted "with satisfaction the progress made by the various Liberation Movements actively engaged in the armed struggle, particularly in Guinea-Bissau, Mozambique, Angola and Namibia, which constitute a major development of far-reaching military, political and social impact on the evolution of the armed liberation struggle."*

## United Nations

From its earliest days the United Nations has dealt with issues of human rights in South Africa. At the second session of the UN General Assembly

---

*African Aims and Attitudes: Selected Documents, edited by Martin Minogue and Judith Molloy (London; Cambridge University Press, 1974), pp. 26–62.

in December 1946, a complaint regarding the denial of human rights to Indian people in South Africa was delivered by Mrs. Pandit of India. As other African nations gained freedom and membership in the UN, and as South Africa repeatedly defied UN jurisdiction over Namibia, a series of resolutions condemning the racism of South Africa and its illegal rule in Namibia were passed by the UN. In 1962 the General Assembly urged that the members of the UN break diplomatic relations with South Africa and that they cease to offer access to their facilities for its planes and ships. In 1963 a Security Council ban (Resolution 181) on sales of arms to South Africa was passed with the United States and Britain both voting for the resolution. A series of further resolutions and debates has followed. In 1979 alone, eighteen resolutions were passed against South African apartheid unanimously or by overwhelming majorities in the UN General Assembly. The General Assembly proclaimed 1982 as the International Year of Mobilization for Sanctions against South Africa.

In addition to the series of resolutions passed by the General Assembly and the Security Council concerning apartheid within South Africa, the UN has focused a great deal of attention on South Africa's administration of Namibia. The historical development of the Namibia problem and early UN action on it are reported in Chapter 3.

In 1973 the General Assembly recognized SWAPO as the authentic representative of the Namibian people. On January 30, 1976 the Security Council adopted Resolution 385, again condemning the illegal control of Namibia by South Africa and calling for "free elections under the supervision and control of the United Nations . . . for the whole of Namibia as one political entity." By 1978 five western nations, Canada, France, the Federal Republic of Germany, the United Kingdom and the United States, brought to the Security Council a report of meetings they had held jointly in South Africa. Resolution 431 was then passed, calling for the appointment of a Special Representative who would ensure that conditions were established for free and fair elections in Namibia, the release of all Namibian political prisoners and return of all refugees and others outside the territory, and a comprehensive cessation of all hostilities with the restriction to base of all South African and SWAPO armed forces.

By September 1978, Resolution 435 established a United Nations Transition Assistance Group for a period of up to twelve months to ensure free elections in Namibia under UN supervision. SWAPO agreed to cooperate fully with these election plans. South Africa agreed in principle, but by October it was clear that South Africa was not prepared to implement 435. Instead, the government proceeded unilaterally, holding elections in Namibia in December, an act condemned subsequently and declared invalid and illegal by the UN General Assembly and the Security Council. This "internal settlement" by South Africa resulted in the Democratic Turnhalle Alliance (DTA) government. The DTA is an alliance of many small, often ethnically based, political parties. The government gives effective control to whites and black minority groups dependent on whites.

In January of 1981, the UN sponsored a conference in Geneva between SWAPO and the South African government to try to negotiate the implementation of Resolution 435. A number of Namibian political parties were represented within the South African delegation. SWAPO again agreed to a cease-fire and an election at any time that would be acceptable to South Africa. The South African delegation was made up largely of DTA members. That delegation refused to take any steps toward implementation of the previous agreement of 435 on the basis that UN supervision was unacceptable because the UN was prejudiced in favor of SWAPO. The conference broke up with nothing accomplished.

Because of South Africa's unwillingness to implement 435, another attempt was made in April of 1981 to have the Security Council impose total sanctions against South Africa. The United States, France and Great Britain joined in the veto of that resolution.

South Africa made extensive military incursions into Angola in August 1981, causing much property damage and, by its own reports, one thousand deaths. Although the invasion was justified by South Africa as an attempt to break up SWAPO guerrilla warfare on the Namibian border, most of the dead were Angolans. In a Security Council effort at condemnation of South Africa's invasion on August 31, the U.S. cast the lone veto.

Incursions into Angola continued in 1982.


## Religious Organizations

In 1954, the World Council of Churches (WCC), without dissent but with a few abstentions, declared segregation based on race, color or ethnic origin to be contrary to the Gospel and incompatible with Christian doctrine and the nature of the Church of Christ. National Church bodies around the world accepted the WCC statement against racism. But there has been a large gap between the acceptance of the statement at the national church level and acceptance by members in local churches. In the U.S., leadership on racial policy in the national denominations was supported by black caucuses of the members, but national church policy has not always been translated into local unity or agreement.

The WCC's efforts for racial justice in South Africa during the 1950s and much of the 1960s were limited to encouraging and assisting South African churches to consult with one another. At that time all of the major denominations in South Africa except the Roman Catholics were members of the WCC. The WCC initiated a worldwide study program on Christian responsibility in areas of rapid social change. One such conference was held in South Africa in December of 1959 with two hundred delegates, only nine of whom came from overseas.

After the Sharpeville Massacre on March 21, 1960 the South African churches, including the three branches of the white Dutch Reformed Church (DRC), requested the WCC to initiate a consultation on Christian responsibility in race relations. The result was the Cottesloe Consultation, where a number of papers prepared in advance by South African churches were discussed. The consultation agreed upon a statement in which many of the participants from diverse points of view felt they had made serious compromises in order to reach a common agreement.

Points made in the statement included: 1) unity in rejecting all unjust discrimination; 2) existence of widely divergent views on apartheid among the groups; 3) agreement that no Christian should be excluded from any church on the grounds of race or colour; 4) agreement that there are no scriptural grounds for the prohibition of mixed marriages; 5) acknowledgement that damage to family life is one deplorable result of migrant labor; 6) agreement that objection to coloured people's participation in Parliament was unfounded. (Indians and Africans were not mentioned as voters or possible members of Parliament.)

The South African government saw the Cottesloe statement as supporting unacceptable changes and immediately denounced it. Thus, the tentative compromise of Cottesloe did not become a starting point for the churches of South Africa to work together on the crisis. Rather, the government pressured all churches to separate from the WCC and prohibited contributions to it. The DRC was urged to sever connections with other Protestant denominations in South Africa. Since the 1970s, WCC personnel have not received visas for entry into South Africa. The DRC isolation was thus reinforced.

By the 1970s, the WCC had become more active and determined in its effort to end apartheid. In 1970 the WCC Program to Combat Racism approved its first grant of $200,000 from specially raised funds, to the educational and humanitarian work of liberation movements of southern Africa. These grants immediately became controversial, not only in South Africa but in many other countries, causing discussion about the acceptability of aid to liberation movements. There was, however, sufficient support within the WCC to continue the grants. African Christians supported the grants, and President Kaunda of Zambia has called the grants a prophetic deed which may well be seen in the future as decisive for the church's fate in southern Africa.

In 1971 the WCC voted overwhelmingly to withdraw its funds from corporations investing or trading in South Africa, South West Africa and the Portuguese African territories. The 250 member churches were urged "to use all their influence, including stockholder action and divestment, to press corporations to withdraw from operations in these countries." South Africa became the focal point for divestment even though the other territories mentioned had not yet become independent. Churches, particularly in England, the Scandinavian countries, West Germany, the Netherlands, New Zealand, Australia, Canada and the United States, undertook divestment activities and campaigns.

The All Africa Conference of Churches, based in Nairobi and comprising most Protestant Church bodies in the continent, has given strong ideological backing to the southern Africa liberation movements. It has taken the position that grants to the liberation movements should not be limited in their designation for humanitarian needs only. The Conference, in continual financial difficulty itself, made some small grants to the liberation movements in the mid-1970s. These grants did not cause any controversy in Africa outside of South Africa.

The British Council of Churches, through its Division of International Affairs, has also been active in relation to South Africa. The BCC recognized a special responsibility in South Africa because of British historical links with it and the key role of British companies currently operating in South Africa. The BCC issued its first report on investment in South Africa in 1973. In 1979 a new report called for economic disengagement, British participation in an international oil boycott against South Africa and British cooperation with (or at least refraining from a veto of) any UN Security Council vote for economic sanctions against South Africa. The 1979 British Council of Churches report was banned in South Africa immediately after its publication.

The National Council of Churches of Christ in the United States has also urged both government and private economic disengagement from South Africa. A detailed policy statement on this was approved in November of 1979. An important avenue of expression for this concern is the Interfaith Center on Corporate Responsibility, in which 180 Roman Catholic orders and dioceses participate, along with seventeen Protestant denominations. The Center provides research, assistance and the stimulus for divestment and for related stockholders' resolutions.

## Corporations

Multinational corporations do not rank high as agents of political and social change. They place a high value on stability, not change, within the countries where they operate. Nevertheless, because of their presence in South Africa, multinational corporations have become a major arena of contention as the citizens of the western world seek ways to oppose apartheid effectively.

Multinational corporations operating in South Africa have faced a new kind of instability: protests by consumers and stockholders in their home countries. Banks have been a prime target because they have made loans directly to the South African government and government controlled corporations called parastatals.* Such loans involve banks dealing heavily in the South African economy and in direct support of the government. Between 1974 and 1976 bank lending to South Africa tripled, reaching $7.6 billion, with U.S. banks contributing about one-third of the total. Many campaigns have been waged to encourage U.S. corporations and banks operating in South Africa to use their influence to bring changes to that society. Between 1977 and 1979 a number of major American lenders to South Africa changed their policies, often in response to those campaigns, either withdrawing altogether, stopping future lending or specifying that they would make no additional loans to enterprises in support of apartheid policies and discriminatory practices.**

In 1972 a series of articles by Adam Raphael on the reprehensible labor policies of many British firms operating in South Africa aroused considerable public concern. This concern was taken up by the Labour Government then in power in the United Kingdom. The result was a Code of Conduct in Industry and Commerce which was followed by a number of other codes.

In early 1977 Reverend Leon Sullivan, a black minister from Philadelphia who is Director of the Opportunities Industrialization Center and a member of the Board of General Motors Corporation, set forth six principles to guide U.S. corporations operating in South Africa. These ask for: (1) nonsegregation of races in all facilities, (2) equal and fair employment practices for all employees, (3) equal pay for equal work, (4) training programs for blacks for skilled positions, (5) increases in the number of blacks in supervisory positions, and (6) improvements outside the work environment in housing, transportation, schooling and other aspects of living conditions. The principles include a responsibility to negotiate with black labor unions.

About one-third of U.S. corporations operating in South Africa have suscribed to the Sullivan principles, but this number covers well over one-half of the labor force employed by U.S. companies there. Leon Sullivan and several agencies have tried to monitor compliance with the principles, although it has proven to be a difficult task. The Sullivan principles are voluntary, but even if enforcement were possible, they are not designated to change the political philosophy of the South African regime. They improve

---

*The major South African parastatals are ARMSCOR, for the production of military armaments; ISCOR for iron and steel production; ESCOM, the production of electricity including nuclear power; SAR&H, railway and harbor operations; SENTRACHEM, chemical production; SASOL, highly secret oil from coal production and possibly the production of nuclear weapons. (From Maketla & Seidman, "U.S. Transnational Corporations' Involvement in South Africa's Military-Industrial Complex", *U.S. Military Involvement in South Africa.*)

**Robert Rotberg, *Suffer the Future: Policy Choices in Southern Africa,* (Cambridge: Harvard University Press, 1980), pp. 130–31.

the economic status of black workers, thereby partially undercutting the economic foundation of apartheid.

In June 1977 the European Economic Community Council of Ministers announced a code of conduct for European Economic Community (EEC) companies, which included urging companies to recognize black trade unions and to bargain collectively with them. The EEC takes no role in monitoring the effectiveness of its code.

The campaign to improve the status of blacks in the workplace has resulted in a number of such codes, perhaps as many as twenty. These codes have remained controversial among the opponents of apartheid, because they do not deal with the basic problem of the sharing of political power. The codes are seen by many persons to be a distraction from the main issue and an instrument for some to use as a substitute for facing up to that main issue.

### Divestment

Limits on the potential for bringing fundamental change within South Africa by making changes within corporate operations has led to discussion regarding ways to effect change from outside that society. Arguments are made for and against the withdrawal of investments and loans by corporations and banks in South Africa and the sale of holdings in such corporations by individuals and organizations. Involvement in the South African economy reaches broadly into U.S. life through investments, loans and trade. Discussions of divestment and sanctions have been an important focus of attention for people concerned about the South African system. The term "divestment" is used comprehensively here to apply to withdrawal of funds and withdrawal from other activity in the economy whether by individuals or corporations.

Divestment merits special attention because it involves a large number of United States citizens in the moral dilemmas of South African society. While most people in the U.S. do not eat South African lobster tails or buy Krugerrands, they do profit directly or indirectly from the economy of South Africa. They may own stock in companies that do business there, be employed in institutions that hold such stocks, may receive benefits from pension funds that hold stock in companies with South African investments, or they may have accounts in banks that make loans to South Africa. U.S. trade with South Africa, both imports and exports, helps the U.S. economy, and few Americans are entirely outside of this system of relationships.

### Arguments Against Economic Pressure

An important argument against outside imposition of economic pressures on South Africa is that such action will bring increased—in fact, the greatest—hardship to those who are already suffering, the blacks. In 1980 the AFSC visitors to South Africa had many opportunities to talk with blacks about this issue. Often, in these conversations, the statement of Chief Albert Luthuli was quoted:

> Economic boycott of South Africa will entail undoubted hardships for Africans. We do not doubt that. But if it is a method which shortens the day of bloodshed, the suffering to us will be a price we are willing to pay. In any case, we suffer already, our children are often undernourished, and on a small scale, so far, we die at the whim of a policeman.

The present suffering and continual uncertainty make additional suffering almost irrelevant and even welcome, if the right change is brought by it. An African woman made the same point to the AFSC visitors when she said, "When you are already on the floor, you don't have very far to fall."

It is true that some Africans oppose divestment because of their marginal existence, which makes the loss of a job a catastrophe for their familes. The government encourages this opposition, and some leaders such as Lucy Mvubelo, General Secretary of the National Union of Clothing Workers, are given wide exposure in South Africa and abroad speaking against divestment. Others oppose it for reasons having to do with their own roles in the present system. In desperation, however, more blacks urge divestment, stressing their willingness to take the consequences of this action which they see as supportive of their cause. In fact, many now suffer for this position.

Yet, there is a long list of black leaders and organizations that are advocates of divestment. The African National Congress, the Pan Africanist Congress, the South African Student Organization, the Black People's Convention, the Coloured Labor Party and the South African Congress of Trade Unions are all on record favoring a withdrawal of foreign investment funds.

It isn't easy for Quakers, who have seen suffering, malnutrition and starvation in South Africa and in other parts of the world, to advocate a policy that might unintentionally add anyone to the roster of the unemployed. It is possible that withdrawal of some foreign firms from complicity in the system of apartheid would have some such effect. Loss of a job can, under the South African system, result in a worker and his family being deported ("endorsed out") to an impoverished "homeland," where economic livelihood is practically nonexistent. Thus advocacy of divestment, even if seen as only symbolic, carries moral obligations to assist South African organizations such as the SACC, SAIRR, Black Consciousness Movement and Quaker Service to cope with any "new" victims of a system that must be abolished. The protests from the economic side must be sufficiently effective to cause the authorities seriously to transform their policies and practices.

An argument against divestment frequently put forward by white South Africans is that liberalizing change can come to South Africa only under conditions of rapid economic growth. Such growth, with the stable base it requires, can be assured only if foreign investments remain steady and secure. There is clearly some truth to this; in most societies it is easier for people to find ways to include previously excluded groups in jobs, housing, income growth, and other benefits when the economy is expanding rather than unstable or contracting. But the record of South Africa on this point is not convincing. With the strong economic growth of the past three decades, apartheid has not lessened; it has in many ways become harsher (see Chapter 2). Economic growth has not brought the social changes expected by its advocates.

Another argument opposing divestment is that if U.S. companies withdraw, others will replace them, possibly with worse treatment for black workers. From a moral standpoint, one should not continue to do wrong to keep someone else from doing the same thing. While the replacement by others is possible, the reasoning underestimates the psychological impact of U.S. withdrawal as seen by other foreign investors. Indeed, the agitation for divestment is stronger in Europe than it is in the United States.

Some even argue that the ending of foreign investment would increase the likelihood of war; thus, those who are opposing investment are accused of "favoring violence." The premise for this argument is that opportunities for increased jobs and income for blacks come through increased investment and industrialization. If such opportunities are not provided, it is said, there would be more unemployed, starving blacks both in bantustans and the African townships around cities. At the same time, it is believed that Afrikaners would be forced into a greater siege mentality and become even less willing to make concessions. The result, the argument goes, would be civil war. Even if the black majority does gain power, the productive system would be a shambles, and the people would be worse off than ever. Those who take this view often overlook the form of civil war that already exists. Violence is currently high, with both sides armed and increasingly so (see Chapter 4). Sabotage, major protests and disruptions are on the rise and will inevitably become even more prevalent unless the apartheid system is abandoned. The AFSC condones neither the increasing violence of the liberation struggle nor the continuing violent repression by the South African government. A realistic assessment compels us to note that while corporate investment, trade and loans may bring some improvements these changes are not now rapid enough or basic enough to avert the increased violence.

The South African government has created many barriers to foreign divestment. In addition to stringent laws prohibiting its advocacy, regulations practically embargo the repatriation of capital from the country if corporations elect to withdraw. Assets must go into Rands purchasing state bonds that mature in seven to fifteen years. Only the interest may be taken out of the country. Corporations may get around this through the transfer by sale of their enterprise on the international stock exchange (assuming they can find a satisfactory buyer). Alternatively, they can continue operations through the device of licensing a subsidiary South African business entity. Some Japanese firms are doing this. Local workers in the South African Firestone plant are reported to be very unhappy with the corporation's decision to license a South African company whose personnel policies are retrogressive. Other companies are moving their registry to Bermuda to escape pressure.

Earlier Swedish positions favoring divestment have been modified following investigations of a trade mission. American firms are sounding out government officials on the possibility of compensation for anticipated losses, should they divest. A French business report early in 1982 suggested that French companies could safely operate in South Africa for only five more years. After that, financial risks would become too great.

It is understandable the American corporate leaders are uncertain and confused by demands for profits and pressures from concerned stockholders. The moral argument remains, and the psychological impact of withdrawals on the country's risk rating cannot be overlooked.

### Arguments for Economic Pressure

Many arguments for divestment and for sanctions against South Africa are put in terms of disrupting its economy effectively enough to cause the government to change its policy of apartheid. But effectiveness is difficult to predict or assure. A good case can be made that apartheid is costly to South Africa's economy and that the country's growth and prosperity would be significantly improved if apartheid were abolished. The South African economy needs more skilled workers and more affluent consumers, both of whom are restricted by the education and employment practices of apartheid. Nonetheless, apartheid continues. Apartheid is motivated by more than profitability; even if it could be conclusively demonstrated that profits would be higher without it, many white South Africans still would hold to the beliefs which underlie apartheid. It is not clear that an economy, particularly one as strong as South Africa's, suffers in the long run from having investment and trade withdrawn. If the idea is to pressure the government of South Africa to change by economic withdrawal, that government may become ever more able to resist outside pressure as it relies less and less on outside economic support. For these reasons, we believe that arguments for divestment that are based on effectiveness are not the strongest arguments.

Many concerned people argue for partial or selective divestment and sanctions. They suggest that companies that fail to live up to the Sullivan principles, banks directly supporting the South African government, or companies involved in military and security operations should become targets of withdrawal. Oil is fequently seen as a prime target for sanctions. These examples are all valid points for protest and pressure for change, but there are two main difficulties with selective economic action. First, the complexity of the changing economic scene makes it very difficult to distinguish fairly among companies in disparate operations. Second, even if it were possible to do so, it is not clear that the impact would be as significant as that of a more comprehensive action.

Others suggest a more positive selective approach. They point out that investment in institutions specifically directed at black development might help in a more fundamental sense to support strength in that community and bring change. While this idea holds clear merit, it has seemed impractical because of the difficulty of identifying circumstances where such support could be meaningful. Under the laws on land and holding titles, blacks in South Africa can provide little security in exchange for loans of capital to begin businesses. Few U.S. banks, for example, have provided capital for the African bank or insurance company established by the African Chamber of Commerce (NAFCOC) led by Sam Motsuenyane. Few are offering soft loans for African entrepreneurs wishing to get started. What does seem clear is that a time will come when investment, loans, and other forces of economic engagement and support will be terribly important in helping build a new South African society based on equality of opportunity and increased justice for all of its citizens.

A stronger argument for divestment involves the message—moral, political and economic—that such an action would communicate both to the current South African government and business communities and to the black people of South Africa. To the ruling Afrikaner minority the message would be: "The system of apartheid is so reprehensible that we shall, ourselves, lose profits we have enjoyed in relation with you and utterly withdraw until apartheid is dismantled. At that time, we shall gladly rejoin with your and others who would then share your power and economy to support the variety of economic enterprises that are benefical to us both."

To the oppressed majority, the message would be one of solidarity. We would be saying that we shall take as drastic an economic action as is possible to help change the system of oppression.

Leon Sullivan understands a progression from codes and partial divestment to more comprehensive actions. In September he said,

> I will be supporting selective divestments against American companies that do not cooperate with the principles, and who fail to comply favorably with their implementation. I will be 'calling for' and urging strong U.S. government action against them, including tax penalties, sanctions and loss of government contracts. And, *if change does not come fast enough,* I will consider

stronger measures, including total divestment and ultimately total embargo on all American exports and imports to and from South Africa.*

Finally, the strongest argument in favor of divestment is a moral one. To be engaged in making a profit of any sort in South Africa is to be making a profit from an immoral and unjust system of oppression. The same argument is true for other economic relationships, such as the purchase of South African products.

All businesses in South Africa, whether they operate under the Sullivan principles or invest in black enterprises or not, are inhibited in openly opposing the political, legal and social framework of apartheid. They are actually co-opted by the South African government, under some conditions becoming part of the enforcing mechanisms of police and army. The National Key Points Act requires companies to take security precautions, such as storing weapons and communications equipment and training and organizing reserve units to guard national "key points" against any protestors or other interference. The large U.S. enterprises involved in fields such as energy, computers and electronics come under the definition of key point: "any place or area so important that its loss or damage, disruption or immobilization may prejudice the Republic or wherever [the Minister of Defense] considers it necessary for the safety of the Republic." Thus U.S. enterprises are pulled into the South African defense mechanisms and are indirectly involved in supporting the system. Moreover, by proclaiming an emergency, the government can order any company in South Africa to produce what the country needs for defense. A company producing passenger cars may find itself producing tanks, jeeps or armored cars. The blueprints for such retooling are already in hand. It is impossible to be in, but not of, the apartheid system. Therefore, a decision about divestment or about sanctions is made finally in terms of the morality of involvement in apartheid.

At some point, we are compelled to abandon our attempts to measure the balance between the good that can be done by continuing to remain linked to the South African economy and the harm that may be done by withdrawing. We simply decide that we must withdraw. This was the moral basis for the action of the American Friends Service Committee when in 1978 it decided to sell its stock in corporations doing business in South Africa. It has been the motivation for many other organizations and individuals who have taken such action. This moral step conveys, in the strongest possible terms, the message of efforts at noncomplicity with the system of apartheid. This step need not separate us from any of the people of South Africa as we distinguish between people and a system which is detrimental to them all.

---

*From a lecture at the University of Witwatersrand, Johannesburg, Sept. 4, 1980.

The owning of company stocks does not involve a personal relationship with either management or labor. AFSC urges the continuing and the building of personal relationships.


**Liberation Groups**

Liberation groups within South Africa and in exile clearly carry a heavy responsibility for altering the course of South African history. Liberation movements have held out a vision of a nonvindictive society of equals that could have led their white adversaries to accept a different future. They continue both to struggle and to articulate their vision of a nonracial society within which all can contribute their skills and talents.

A number of South African groups working for liberation operate in exile. Two of these are the well-known liberation movements: the African National Congress (ANC), with headquarters in Lusaka, and the Pan Africanist Congress (PAC), with its headquarters in Dar es Salaam. They have offices and staff in a number of cities, including London and New York. They both have official observer status at the United Nations and are recognized and supported by the Organization of African Unity (OAU). Humanitarian aid for refugees and for scholarships is provided by the liberation movements with help from the UN Educational and Training Program for Southern Africa, the UN High Commission for Refugees, the World Council of Churches, and the All-African Conference of Churches and other groups. Aid in the form of arms and training for guerrillas is offered by some nations.

These liberation movements play important roles in the struggle for justice and freedom. First, they provide a platform from which African nationalists may speak to the world, particularly in the forum of the United Nations, since people within South Africa can speak out in this manner only at severe risk. Second, the liberation movements provide a sense of history, pride and encouragement to many South Africans who desire radical change in their country, whether they are actively involved in work for that change or not. Third, the liberation movements provide training and experience. Some leaders gain important administrative and organizing experience. Others achieve advanced education degrees.

As stated in Chaper 4, the liberation movements have accepted armed struggle as necessary. They offer explicit guerrilla and sabotage training and provide personnel, arms and material for infiltration back into South Africa. The successful armed struggles in Guinea-Bissau, Angola, Mozambique and, most recently, Zimbabwe have lent credence for many persons to the claims that the only option for black South Africans is guerrilla warfare. Recent history provides examples of people's forces overcoming highly skilled armies equipped with sophisticated weapons: Vietnam and Iran are two. The additional lesson from Zimbabwe, that after armed battles it is possible to establish peace with justice for blacks and whites, increases the persuasiveness of the claim.

There are other liberation groups based outside South Africa, without the formal status of the liberation movements. The Black Consciousness Movement (BCM), founded by Steve Biko, found it necessary to operate in exile after October 1977, when most of its organizations and leaders were banned in South Africa. While many members are affiliated with ANC or PAC, a major thrust of BCM is for greater unity and cooperation among the liberation movements.

Small groups of white war resisters who have left South Africa also contribute to the overall antiapartheid movement and to the work for change in South Africa. The Unity Movement, an early attempt to build opposition on nonracial lines, is also based outside the country.

External groups have ties with groups inside the country, some underground and others open and legal. There is a wide variety of these, ranging from organizations of black workers, registered and unregistered unions, to the South African Council of Churches, to AZAPO (the Azanian People's Organization, similar to the former Black People's Convention), to the Soweto Committee of Ten, to the Port Elizabeth Black Civic organization. Some are more consciously political than others, but most see the need to cooperate and work together for liberation. The ties between black students, their parents and workers are being strengthened, as boycotts, strikes and demonstrations increase in frequency.

The homeland leaders and blacks who serve in government-created institutions such as the township councils are generally rejected as leaders. They are seen by most blacks as powerless, co-opted by the apartheid system. Considered by some as an exception to this rule is Chief Gatsha Buthelezi of the Zulus, one of the larger ethnic groups in South Africa. He heads Inkatha, founded in 1928 as a Zulu cultural organization, now more a political movement. While open to all Africans, it remains primarily Zulu in its membership, which had reached more than three hundred thousand by mid-1980.* Buthelezi has been openly critical of the government policies, and yet is restrained by them. Relations between Buthelezi and the liberation movement have varied. In 1979 he met with Oliver Tambo in London. Tambo's January 1980 address suggested that ANC questioned the effectiveness of trying to bring change from within the system, but was willing to postpone final judgment until results could be measured. This can be read as acceptance of Buthelezi's role in South Africa. However, ANC sharply condemned Buthelezi in June 1980 when he tried to stop the wave of school boycotts protesting unequal education, and a break became apparent.

---

*South Africa: Time Running Out, p. 194.

Nonetheless, as leader of the Zulus and Inkatha, he has power now, and he remains a potential force for the future majority government era.

The external liberation groups provide a worldwide platform for the goals and aspirations of black South Africans and their allies. They also supply training, experience, arms and equipment, while the internal movements provide immediate experience of the changing conditions, trends and moods within South Africa. They remain in direct contact with those seeking change and those resisting.

Few groups are entirely external or internal, however. There is strong internal support for the liberation groups. But knowledge of the pulse and people of the country is critical for the development of effective strategies and plans. Exile groups face the risk of becoming divorced from the people for whom they work and the internal groups risk co-optation on the one hand and banning, prison or death on the other. Approaches and ideology vary among the internal and external liberation groups. Nevertheless, these groups represent the oppressed people of South Africa and, taken together, are the most important initiators, implementers and evaluators of change in South Africa.

## A Case History

---

### International Pressure Works on South Africa

*On November 26, 1981 forty-four men who called themselves rugby players belonging to the "Ancient Order of Froth Blowers" landed in the Seychelles on a commercial flight from South Africa. Their intentions were disclosed when custom officials found guns beneath toys the Froth Blowers had "brought for poor children." These mercenaries had come to take over the government of the Seychelles. Under whose auspices they came has not been proven, but many persons suspect the South African government.*

*To return to South Africa, the men hijacked an Air India plane. In South Africa, five men were charged with kidnapping, a lesser offense than hijacking in South Africa, and 39 were released.*

*South Africa signed the 1970 Hague Convention which requires that hijackers be prosecuted or extradited. The U.S., Britain, France, West Germany, Italy, Japan and Canada have all agreed to end air links with countries breaching the Hague Convention. This sanction has been invoked against Afghanistan for failure to act in the case of a hijacked Pakistani plane.*

*The U.S. and other Western countries expressed concern, apparently with some vigor, to South Africa for its failure to comply with the Hague Convention and pointed out the inevitable consequences if the hijackers were not prosecuted.*

*On January 4, 1982, South African authorities acted against the entire group of mercenaries, charging them all with hijacking.*

---

# CHAPTER 7

# *The Tenacity of Power and the Pressure for Change*

> At the end of the day I fear that the drama can only be brought to its climax in one of two ways—through the selective brutality of terrorism or the impartial horrors of war.
>
> —Kenneth Kaunda in *The Riddle of Violence*, p. 67.

Kaunda speaks with authority, having led Zambia to independence by a campaign of passive resistance with a minimum of bloodshed. He sees how much more difficult the South African situation is. The American Friends Service Committee still searches, as Kaunda does for the compassionate solution that could bring an end to apartheid without the catastrophe that seems inevitable. Easy but unrealistic solutions will not work as seemingly immovable power is confronted by irresistible pressure for change.

The ruling group shows no sign of relenting. Ominous rumblings on the right, heard in the election of April 1981, have caused the government to slow the pace of even the small reforms it had begun. The election of President Reagan in the U.S. has had a first effect of giving encouragement to a hard line in South Africa. At the same time, the various liberation groups are accelerating the pace of demonstrations and bombings. The tenacity by which the ruling group clings to its position is matched by the increasing pressure for shared power by the excluded majority. It is a polarization which is bound to increase as long as there is no significant change.

## The Tenacity of Power

People do not easily surrender their power or the privilege it brings them. Indeed, the perquisites of privilege are not considered by those who hold them as a coat that can be taken off and generously given away but as the very substance of cultural heritage and values which make life worth living. This is all the more true in South Africa where Afrikaners believe they have a religious mission to hold and control the land. And their determination is strengthened by the fact that they have no alternative European homeland.

The toughness of their security measures is matched by the eagerness of their argued rationalizations. A major justification is the preservation of

103

the ethnic and cultural identities of a diversity of peoples and homelands. In a pamphlet published in January, 1981 and widely circulated by the South African government, Dr. Jan. S. Marais neatly blends the longstanding government policy into the worldwide movement for self-determination:

> ...Throughout the world distinctive national groups are clamouring for their "national identity" and retention of their culture. ... In South Africa, national groups are given the option of ruling themselves as independent nations. American minority groups have never been offered this option. ... And what of the Palestinian paradox? Whilst the world refuses to recognize Transkei, a homeland is urged for the Palestinian people to "give effective expression to a people's national dignity."

Various critics of the government hold a different point of view. The Christian Institute, which has since been banned, said in 1976:

> ... History will judge the homelands policy of the South African Government to be a sham and a fraud designed to perpetuate white domination over the country as a whole, and to provide a pretext for arbitrarily depriving millions of black South Africans of their natural birthright of citizenship in a country whose wealth they have played a major part in creating.

The government continues a policy of deportation to homelands that are poor in resources, poor in land and already crowded with people who are unemployed and often malnourished. Citizenship in the Republic of South Africa is restricted to whites; Africans can have citizenship only in their ghetto homelands.

The application of the principle of cultural separation to their own group—an Afrikaner–Anglo homeland more proportionate to the size of their population, i.e., 16% of the land instead of 87%—is seriously proposed only by a few extremist whites. The driving wheels of industrialization and interdependence have gone too far to make such a solution possible, even if desired.

### Pressure for Change

The main force for change must come from the oppressed people. As they rise to claim their rightful human heritage, the structures of oppression will begin to crumble. Frederick Douglass articulated the militant spirit of the antislavery movement in nineteenth century United States. In a speech in 1857 he said:

> The limits of tyrants are prescribed by the endurance of those whom they oppress. ... If there is no struggle there is no progress. Those who profess to favor freedom and yet depreciate agitation are men who want crops without plowing up the

> ground; they want rain without thunder and lightning. They want
> the ocean without the awful roar of its many waters.*

The continual struggle of blacks in South Africa against the domination of whites has passed through four phases: armed struggle, political resistance, nonviolent struggle, and back to armed struggle.

1. The first phase, sporadic warfare, was nearly ended by 1900.

2. In the latter part of the nineteenth century and the beginning of the twentieth, most of the resistance was political within the legal framework. The normal political techniques of voting, abstaining from voting as protest, petitions, negotiations and other methods were used.

3. From the formation of the ANC in 1912, through Sharpeville in 1960, nonviolent direct action was the primary thrust of black resistance. Demonstrations, marches, sit-ins, pass burnings, civil disobedience and other techniques not usually part of the political process marked the era.

4. Since Sharpeville, armed struggle has been seen by many blacks as a necessary tool for liberation. Armed struggle in this context includes urban guerrilla sabotage, and the arson, looting and destruction of government property, often in the African townships.

The strategies of these four periods overlap, and armed violence is used as part of a total strategy that includes political resistance and nonviolent action. New techniques may be developed, such as the already evident massive attendance at funerals of those killed in the struggle and organizations without leaders who are publicly identifiable. Is it possible for a fifth phase with primary reliance on nonviolent noncooperation to ensue? The possibilities at this time seem dim despite continued widespread use of nonviolent techniques.

### Strategies of Change

Those at a distance cannot dictate strategies of resistance. We recognize this. Our lives are not on the line. We must look to the blacks of South Africa to be the main force for the creation of a more humane order. We can guide the actions that we take in our remoteness, but not the actions of those in the midst of the fray.

The possible responses to this intractable conflict are many, but we must scrutinize them carefully in view of the extreme onesidedness of power. With this in mind we will consider the government actions, the response of various conciliatory forces within the country and proposals for negotia-

---

*Philip S. Foner, ed., *The Life and Writings of Frederick Douglass* (New York: International Publishers, 1950), Vol. 2, p. 437.

tion. We will consider the individual moral approach and the possibilities of collective nonviolent campaigns carried on outside and inside South Africa.

We will appraise these responses with a knowledge that other persons may reach differenct conclusions; that each individual within the society will function in different ways, from apathetic acceptance to open rebellion; that outsiders like ourselves, although limited in our influence, will be freer to follow conscientious leadings because we are not direct participants in either the repression or the humiliation. We will remind ourselves that as Americans or citizens of the western world we are, in spite of ourselves, directly or indirectly involved through many linkages in exploitation. We can only be involved in the movement to remove injustices by breaking through silence and apathy into action.

## Official Responses to the Need for Change

---

**Race Bars in Mines to End**

*The Government has accepted the principle of eliminating race discrimination in the mining industry—but will not amend legislation until measures have been taken to safeguard White miners' jobs.*

*South Africa Digest*
October 9, 1981, p. 3.

---

The ruling powers in South Africa are clearly aware of the need for change, but they insist on controlling the pace and the extent of change in order that it may be, in their terms, "constructive." By this they mean that it will not challenge the power structure.

*South Africa Digest,* a publication of the South African government (June 13, 1980) reported, "steadily, sometimes with a speed that confuses some but pleases most, a new South Africa is being fashioned encompassing the lives of all citizens."

In August 1980, when an AFSC visitor asked a black South African about changes in his country, he shrugged his shoulders and responded wryly, "What changes?" Though the scene is not static and many forces are demanding reform, this was the usual answer from blacks.

When problems are so deep and needed change so far-reaching, the basic question to ask is whether the change proposed in any way leads toward a share of political-economic power for the deprived majority. Small changes to alleviate certain aspects of injustice may be helpful without really challenging the structure. As Bishop Tutu says, these may be just "applying an inhuman system more humanely." The government can be expected to use all kinds of devices to cause division in the liberation movement by favoring one group against another, promoting palliative changes to win over some, and co-opting leaders into privileged positions.

With this perspective in mind, let us look at some examples of changes that have positive aspects but do not go far enough.

—The elimination of the major job reservation law, reserving certain higher paid jobs for whites only, strikes down a racial barrier and is a move in the right direction. But the barriers in custom and practice remain and there is no positive legislation against discrimination.

—For the first time, because of responses to the Wiehahn Commission and a change in the law, labor unions organized by Africans can be registered by the government, a necessary step for official recognition of bargaining powers and the right to strike. This seems to be an advance. But the registration process is complicated and subject to government rejection of the union seeking registration. The government can withdraw registration at any time, and there is no right of appeal. Registration entails disclosure of a great deal of information about the union and its members and may lead to greater control rather than greater freedom. Furthermore, it is against the law for registered unions to participate in political activity. Black labor leaders are perplexed as to the most suitable tactics in response.

—A recent change made in influx control laws arising from the Riekert Commission recommendations was discussed in Chapter 2. Here again, a seemingly more liberal provision has little practical effect.

The South African government has given no indication that it is willing to consult with the real leaders of the suppressed people. Nelson Mandela and many others remain in jail or in exile. The government picks those leaders that it wants to deal with or those it thinks it can control. Such "leaders" represent only a fraction of the population. The rejection by blacks of the South African government's formulation of separated political rights in urban townships, in homelands and in the national government is evident. Most coloureds and Asians rejected participation in the President's Council and probably will have real doubts about P. M. Botha's trial balloon in early 1982 for some form of political representation in the national Parliament. Africans continue to be omitted from the source of real power that affects their lives. Less than six per cent of the eligible voters participated in the Soweto elections in 1978 for the urban council, thanks to an effective campaign against voting. Similarly, Asians in great numbers boycotted the referendum for the government's proposed Asian Council. Earlier, led by the Labour Party, the coloured community made the Coloured Representative Council impotent, and it was finally disbanded. Nothing short of real power sharing among all groups will meet the need. The government has selected leaders in Namibia by establishing the Democratic Turnhalle

Alliance. The glaring failure of the "internal settlement" of Bishop Muzorewa in Zimbabwe stands as an unheeded example. Fundamental change in apartheid will not come in South Africa until those most seriously affected by it have a share in the decision making to eliminate it.

## Conciliating Efforts

Even in the drastic confrontation of forces we have outlined, we do not wish to dismiss efforts of individuals and groups to bridge across the barriers using communication, moral suasion and conciliation. Since the system is based to an extent on biblical interpretation, theological and biblical arguments against apartheid may have effect in some circles and should be strongly promoted. Exposure to outside thinking, insofar as it is possible, is an antidote to narrow-mindedness. Many people in South Africa find themselves in the middle between the ruling group and the afflicted ones. They are strongly against apartheid, but through constraints of job, family and temperament, find it difficult to join a movement of opposition. These persons have on occasion protested harsh actions of authorities, helped families in distress and given succor to persecuted individuals. Anything that can be done to reduce the fears and prejudices of white South Africans, not least those in the government, may help to bring a better future. While such varied overtures by persons doing what they can within the limits confining them are useful, they are not the main thrust against apartheid. They are valid when they promote, but do not inadvertently obstruct, the change that is needed.

## The Place of Negotiation and Mediation in Change

There is an important distinction between bridge-building conciliation within the current structures and negotiation for a redistribution of power. Friends and others who work for a just peace are eager to find ways to substitute negotiation for violent conflict. But in a situation of great inequity such as South Africa, negotiation to stabilize a new balance of power becomes a part of the process of change when the oppressed have gained sufficient strength to obstruct governmental decisions and make their own decisions. When the authority of the government is basically challenged so it is forced to deal with the real leaders of the people and not those of its own choosing, negotiations become meaningful. If prematurely attempted, negotiation and mediation may hinder change by sidetracking the demands of those seeking political power and strengthening the hold of the ruling power. When the opposing forces are more nearly equal, negotiation becomes a pertinent method for bringing about change and finding new political forms.

It is then that third party mediation by offical international or national bodies may become important. The parties in the conflict will still be caught in the hostility and mistrust engendered in the turmoil. The ruling group will still be trying to keep its hold. Each side is likely to say it cannot possibly speak to the other. Each side may still be looking for resources, outside help and collective will to overcome the opponent. The third party, which may be invited or may intervene, can provide an atmosphere of neutrality without ulterior motive, supportive of the process of negotiations and compromise.

Private third parties can facilitate the process of talks if they have the confidence of both sides and can move back and forth with discretion and no publicity. They can carry messages between groups not on speaking terms, convey impressions of the willingness to negotiate and even at times suggest terms. Confidence is not easy to acquire, since third parties cannot be neutral in the face of tyranny. Their sympathies and actions must be clearly on the side of the oppressed, but willingness at all times to speak to those in power can still bring openings.

The lesson of Zimbabwe illustrates these points. Over the years, many attempts at negotiation failed; the illegal UDI regime of Ian Smith was not ready to give up; the opposition forces of ZANU and ZAPU were not strong enough to gain major concessions. The UN sanctions against Southern Rhodesia were one factor in changing the power relationship between blacks and whites. They gave blacks a sense of international support and encouragement while causing difficulties for the Smith government. At the stage when guerrilla forces controlled large parts of the population by night while the Rhodesian armed forces maintained sporadic control by day, the ruling group came to realize that they were trying to defend a political order, namely white supremacy, which no longer existed and could not be restored.

In April 1979 in a last minute effort to retain some power, the government held elections which were boycotted by the two liberation movements. Bishop Muzorewa, one of the African leaders who had agreed to the elections, became Prime Minister, but Smith's Rhodesian Front party retained the major controls, giving currency to the phrase "internal settlement." The new government was not recognized by the international community and the civil war continued.

Commonwealth heads of government meeting in Zambia in August, 1979 worked out the Lusaka Accord, which envisaged a process of peaceful transition to majority rule through supervised elections. In accordance with the terms of the Lusaka agreement, the British Government convened a constitutional conference at Lancaster House, London in September, 1979.

Among other groups, the American Friends Service Committee and Quaker Peace and Service of London were able to play a minor role. Because they had kept in touch with liberation leaders over the years they could facilitate communication among participants on the fringes of the very difficult negotiations which set the stage for a new order. Elections were held, supervised by British authorities. The old order leaders and their allies, including South Africa, fully expected that the government of Muzorewa would win. The balloting was carefully safeguarded by civil servants and monitored by a host of foreign correspondents and a Commonwealth Observer Group. The people showed unmistakably that the guerrilla leaders, Robert Mugabe and Joshua Nkomo, were their choice.

## Individual Conscience and Social Change

Much religious thought and faith emphasizes individual morality as the primary response to social evil. An individual may sell his or her stock in a multinational corporation operating in South Africa, because it is wrong to make profit from exploitation. The personal pacifist refuses to participate in war. Such actions are not necessarily based on a calculation of consequences or a tally of beneficial results. By themselves these actions will not end apartheid or stop war. The moral witness says, "I do what I must do and leave the rest to God."

This personal position has validity and frequently embodies a degree of commitment that is important in social change movements. In South Africa courageous young whites are refusing to participate in the military. Some are going to jail, others are leaving the country. If such action becomes contagious and many are moved to do the same things the movement may have social effect. It has had social impact in causing churches and the government to give serious consideration to conscientious objection to war.

A variant of the personal approach is the strategy of converting the leaders of an evil government. The thought is that if only the few responsible can be brought to see the light then a transformation will be accomplished. Power and privilege in South Africa are held not just by a few individuals but in varying degrees by a whole class of people, defined by skin color, whose lives are inextricably bound up to the status quo. They are all children of God. They think of themselves as estimable fathers and mothers, warmhearted, generous, hard-working, courageous and strong. The Afrikaners think they are inheritors of a noble tradition which they must protect. But they are caught in a rigid circle of self-confirming action and logic which leads them to think their advantaged position is sacrosanct. Such people, however well-meaning and sincere, are not easily open to persuasion.

The hard truth is that confrontation and resistance are necessary for a reallocation of power. A few may be converted, but their transformation puts them beyond the pale of their own society—shunned, banned, or exiled. Such is the fate of the former head of the Christian Institute, Beyers Naude. His heroic witness will someday be vindicated, but for now it has produced but a small dent in the armor of apartheid. Individual conversions are an inspiration to many and have some cumulative effect, but the oppressed people cannot be expected to wait until a large enough number of the oppressors have seen their error and embraced drastic change. This personal approach is not an adequate answer to an aroused people in a desperate situation. It can readily become an excuse for inaction. Lucretia Mott, the nineteenth century Quaker leader in the abolitionist and women's movements said, "Any great change must expect opposition because it shakes the very foundation of privilege," and later, "We are not to wait until all are converted to pure nonresistance any more than we had to wait for all to be made antislavery in heart."*

## Nonviolent Direct Action

The individual conscience propelled by its own inner dynamic has often moved on from a personal stand to inspire collective resistance. The difficult questions remain with the participants in group action. There is no litmus test for any action to determine the degree of physical or psychological violence within it. Those working on a strategy for nonviolent struggle must also face the question of effectiveness, as well as the question of how the particular strategy suits their value judgment on nonviolence. Gwendolen Carter says of violence in South African society that it "is so porvasive that it almost ceases to be noticeable except when a well know person is affected or the circumstances are so unusual as to attract attention."**

In the atmosphere of spiralling violence in South Africa described here, it may be chimerical to look for a return to nonviolent struggle as the primary method of working for liberation. Yet, such a turn could be an important key to a compassionate solution which would benefit all, blacks as well as whites.

Even as we say this we must acknowledge that the discipline of nonviolence does not come easily. A violent reaction on the part of an affronted person is commonly seen as self-defense and an assertion of dignity. Nonviolent resistance must be much more studied and planned. Many will find it easier to fight back than to accept suffering and turn it into a challenge to the conscience of others. In a nonviolent campaign feelings of wrath must be transmuted into resistance which minimizes the spirit of revenge. Those already suffering are required to stand up before batons and gunfire without hurling brickbats and broken bottles at the users of armed force.

---

*Lucretia Mott Speaking,* compiled by Margaret Hope Bacon, Pendle Hill Pamphlet #234 (Wallingford, Pa.: Pendle Hill Publications, 1980), pp.18, 22.

**Carter, Gwendolen M., *Which Way Is South Africa Going?* Bloomington, Ind.: Indiana University Press, 1980, p.12.

The argument for nonviolent resistance is that people, with only their bare hands, have a monopoly of moral force, even though the governing power has a monopoly on weapons of suppression. Moral force is enhanced by a movement which relies on the power of love rather than the power to kill.

The South African government presents a classic example of bureaucracy, musclebound with arms and ideologically ill-equipped to meet the challenge of massive, nonviolent noncooperation. The government has already demonstrated an inability to use its bludgeoning techniques to foreclose strikes involving even a relatively small geographic area and a relatively small number of workers. What would happen if the black workers, servants and farm laborers withdrew cooperation on a massive scale in a well organized nonviolent campaign!

Is it possible that at a certain point, as Kaunda puts it, the oppressor will realize that "he is powerless, in the last resort, to prevent the inevitable, because he is trying to fight not an army but an idea, and short of exterminating a whole population he cannot bomb or blast it out of their minds?" The truth of the idea—the releasing of thirty million people to be human—is better served by nonviolent actions which do not deny the basic humanity of the oppressor. May there be a moment of truth when the South African rulers find that the rigid confining fabric of apartheid is stretched so far that it breaks, and there is a resolution in the highest circles to free all the South African people from bondage and devote the immense resources of South Africa toward the development of all of southern Africa? We cannot be optimistic, but neither can we dismiss such a possibility.

The keys to successful organization of a nonviolent campaign are an awakened people and skilled leaders. All leaders must understand the use of nonviolent techniques and must be willing to suffer. They must believe that they can convince their opponents to change their ways more forcefully by nonviolent action than by killing and maiming. The people must become alert, aroused to the necessity for struggle, mobilized, disciplined to work together and to forego retaliation. Three well-known South African leaders with great potential for nonviolent leadership have all died: Sobukwe of PAC and Luthuli of ANC while restricted, and Biko of the Black Consciousness Movement while in police custody. New leaders develop in the squatters' movements, school boycotts and trade unions and keep a low profile in the emerging style of organization.* Much of the current antigovernment activity is nonviolent, but it seems to lack cohesion and close commitment to the aim of transforming the system without annihilating its proponents.

---

*"Between January and March 1973, African workers seeking higher wages struck approximately 150 Natal firms one after another without any apparent overall organization or even obvious leaders." Ibid, p. 93.

The precedent of Gandhi's work in India and the Defiance Campaign in South Africa are a vivid part of the heritage.

The evaluation of the effectiveness of acts of resistance often differs among participants and among observers. The anti-pass laws demonstration at Sharpeville, which cost seventy lives, visibly shook the government of South Africa. Because of the deaths and the lack of change in the pass laws, the demonstration was called a failure by the liberation movement, justifying a move to guerrilla warfare. On the other hand, the guerrilla warfare on the Namibian border, which has cost thousands of lives, seems to have done little to move South Africa but is not called a failure.

The philosophy of nonviolent struggle is not based on comparative death counts, but rather on the possibility of redeeming a sick society through suffering. The acts of confrontation and disobedience are directed against a system and not against a people. The hope is to win over the oppressors by "soul-force" or "love-force." The power and riches of the ruling groups are predicated on the coerced consent of the oppressed. If this consent is replaced by active resistance, power and privilege eventually collapse, making way for a new order to emerge.

## The Challenge of South Africa to Nonviolence

Even as we call upon others to consider the possibilities of nonviolence in their struggle for transforming change in South Africa, we recognize that it is a setting that poses great challenges and deep questions to our beliefs, convictions and commitments. Indeed, we are convinced that there is a message for us in the South African situation, a calling to us to look more deeply at the meaning of our own belief in the ultimate power and rightness of nonviolence in all struggles for humane social change. So we speak to ourselves as well as to others. We try to listen as fully as we can, especially when we consider the implications of a predominantly white, essentially protected group of Americans calling upon a black, beleaguered community to consider nonviolence, to consider taking even more violence upon themselves, to consider sparing their white oppressors the searing fires of armed violence in return.

When we listen, we find that wherever we have turned the basic message seems to be the same, especially as we encounter those men and women who are committed to the need for fundamental transformation and the rise of the black majority to its rightful role in the recreation of their tortured nation. They say to us and to the world, "In the face of the violent repression of the unjust South African regime, there is no alternative to the use of selective, responsibly chosen but widespread armed struggle." Many persons inside and outside of South Africa say this with deep regret, for they know the cost of a revolution that turns to armed violence as one of its key tactics, but they are also convinced that through such a choice the way may be opened toward a new society.

As we face this challenge to our own nonviolent position we may too easily be pinning our hopes on bridge building and conciliation, personal witness and negotiation. Even when we are pushed forward to the idea of nonviolent struggle, do we deal adequately, compassionately, and honestly either with our own commitments or with the agonized situation of our sisters and brothers, black and white, in South Africa? We are forced to take a deeper look at our own experiences. They offer us a very limited sense of what it means to be committed to nonviolence in a struggle for fundamental, radical change on a national scale.

Our struggle has been different. By and large, when we refer to nonviolent movements, we usually think of our own most recent U.S. experiences with the struggles for racial justice, for peace and for women's rights. For the most part, we have defined these as confrontations in which we were pressing our own nation and its leaders to live up to the country's best ideas, to enforce its constitution, to carry out certain selective structural changes that would be in line with what we understood to be the best democratic visions of our society.

Thus when we speak of nonviolent action, we have generally envisioned legally sanctioned marches and other peaceful demonstrations, selective boycotts and civil disobedience—almost always with a limited risk of either extensive jail sentences or of official violence. When we returned home after a day, a week or a month of such action, almost never have we had to consider such possibilities as midnight knocks at the door, police detention without charges, banning, lifelong imprisonment or death.

One of our most recent experiences with something broader and deeper came in the fifties and sixties when the U.S. black southern movement confronted the state and local governments of its region. The cruelty of police and white mobs in some of those situations was a small indication of what one can expect in South Africa. U.S. demonstrators were almost always able to look to the federal government for protection against the worst assaults of violent repression. Rarely, if ever, in our experience have we engaged in or seen a massive, sustained nonviolent campaign that challenged the legitimacy, authority and political basis of the national government itself. We tend to be insulated against a sense of what might really be involved in such a campaign. Our imagination too often fails us when we are called upon to consider what might be the costs, the implications and the furor—as well as the blessings—of such nonviolence.

If we want to speak responsibly of nonviolence when we think of a situation like South Africa, if we want to be more than sounding brass and tinkling cymbals when we announce our commitment to nonviolence in the face of the South African government's massive system of sophisticated, violent coercion, then we must at least stretch our imaginations and broaden the arena of our vicarious experience.

Our own national history reminds us that this country's colonial leaders chose armed rebellion as the way to break out of British domination, which in comparison to the South African situation seems gentle and beneficent. Even then there were Quakers who paid the price with their possessions and their freedom for refusal to pay taxes for that war or to support it in other ways. We must remember also that the entrenchment and protection of the system of slavery in our constitution and in our social and economic arrangements made radical abolitionism a dangerous vocation. To oppose slavery required in many cases a lifelong commitment to civil disobedience, a readiness to face the terrible onslaughts of mobs and a commitment to persevere until death. We must recognize that slavery was finally broken not only by heroic, nonviolent action on the part of blacks and whites, but also through the bloodshed of a civil war that was primarily fought to preserve the union. We recognize the bitter legacy of that war which ended the institution of slavery but not its roots of racism.

There was a massive, essentially nonviolent movement for the recreation of American society after the Civil War. Black people, with a relatively small band of allies, were determined to press beyond the broken shackles of slavery and move to create a new society. They sought one in which the dehumanizing power of white supremacy would be broken, where blacks and whites would participate equally in the political redevelopment of at least the southern region and at best the entire nation.

Such a vision challenged the assumptions and white supremacist convictions of the vast majority of the nation, including the leadership of the federal government, and the newly freed black community had to deal with that reality. Moreover, in Mississippi and South Carolina the former slaves were a majority, and in scores of counties throughout the southern Black Belt they were present in proportions quite similar to those in South Africa. Their numbers and their vision threatened the whites of the region who were supported by the whites of their nation. This fundamentally nonviolent black movement, begun in the first decade after the civil war, was betrayed and buried for half a century, largely through the force of white arms and the coercive uses of white economic power. In the course of more than a decade of struggle thousands of black persons lost their lives, and tens of thousands more were hounded out of the region. When we consider the extent of that crushing, bloody repression of an essentially unarmed force seeking basic transformation of the political and economic order, we must surely move with a deep sense of humility and trepidation as we express our belief in nonviolence for other lands.

The important point in all this is the realization that we have some models in our own society of mass, nonviolent campaigns for fundamental change. Each was born of the time and circumstance, rather than based on a spiritual commitment to nonviolence. But it may be that until we believers develop such nonviolent campaigns we shall need to work with the less-than-perfect models that history has presented to us. Properly apprehended through the eyes of compassion, these historical examples, like the ones from our own recent times, must certainly engage our minds and hearts as we consider the meaning of nonviolence for transformation in South Africa.

Moving beyond our own shores, it is obvious that the one national non-violent, revolutionary struggle that is a model to follow is that of India during the decades of Gandhi's *Satyagraha* movement. Unquestionably, here is an example that brings much hope to us about the possibilities of national, mass nonviolent struggle for freedom. At the same time, we have learned that we must not be facile or simplistic in the attempt to glean its lessons and inspirations for South Africa.

Gandhi was not faced with an entrenched white settler population that was determined to rule India as its own homeland. The British center of power and decision making was thousands of miles away, and India was only a part of its extended colonial empire. The British government sent subalterns—brutal ones as well as humane ones—to deal with the Indian movement. In the case of South Africa, white resistance is right there, entrenched on the land that each party claims as its home. The weapons of repression are in full supply right there, along with the troops.

Comparatively, the goals of the Indian movement, like those of similar anticolonial struggles elsewhere, were simple: the removal of British rule. In South Africa, the heart of the affair is much more complex, and thus the struggle is much more explosive. While they proved themselves quite capable in the uses of violence, coercion and brutality, the British did not reach the South African levels of sophistication in the uses of organized, repressive force.

Nevertheless, even though the Indian struggle was simpler to carry out, it required decades of continuing sacrificial nonviolent action and tremendous demands on the lives of all participants. Nor was it without outbursts of violence coming from the gut-level impatience of the people. Although the struggle for independence was successful, the tragedies of the Muslim/ Hindi split, the assassination of the Mahatma and the fundamental confusion of much of the nonviolent leadership after his death show that the positive aims of a nonviolent movement are not easy to attain.

In this context, we have also pondered the surprising examples of Zimbabwe and Iran, trying to understand what they teach us about our assumptions concerning nonviolence. Generally, in our linear view of life, we have assumed that nonviolent means lead to nonviolent ends, and that violence begets violence.

We look at Zimbabwe and note with wonder and profound gratitude the fact that Robert Mugabe, a Marxist, who led the armed, black guerrilla movement against the unjust white minority government of Rhodesia, is now risking his life and his reputation to develop a society based on reconciliation, forgiveness and nonracial leadership. In doing so he has chosen to challenge and defy some who were his closest comrades and companions in the long, hard military campaign. This does not fit into our easy categories of cause and effect, of means and ends.

In Iran the national struggle to depose the Shah faced all the terror of his American supplied military equipment and was a largely unarmed, religiously motivated mass uprising of the people. Millions risked their lives in the struggle for a new order; thousands lost their lives in what was at times a highly disciplined campaign. Now, that once unarmed movement has disintegrated into a reign of fear, terror and death for many of its own people, perhaps because there was no unity in the people's vision of the new society. Again, this does not fit our assumptions of cause and effect.

We consider all these things as we probe the meaning of South Africa for any search for nonviolent, transforming compassionate action. We ask whether we have soberly, honestly considered the massive commitment of life, energy, imagination and determination that will be required to carry out a truly just revolution in South Africa. In the light of our government's support of South Africa's oppressors, in the light of our government's fundamental reliance on violence for national security, in the light of our nation's own long list of fundamental, unsettled business regarding racial and economic injustice, in the light of our own participation in this government and in this nation, our South African brothers and sisters, although too polite to do so, have every right to ask us: "When will your cherished faith in nonviolence manifest itself in the works of nonviolent transformation on behalf of your own nation, on behalf of our people, on behalf of a threatened world?"

We must be prepared at least to hear that question, at least to ponder its meaning for our lives and our institutions. For those who are prepared to move forward into a more active response, a challenge comes from the long-term American civil rights leader Muhammed Isaiah Kenyatta. He calls on American Christians and "others who have ears" to carry out nonviolent acts of imaginative and symbolic civil disobedience against the evil of apartheid and U.S. complicity in it.* Kenyatta says the campaign could begin with small groups who are ready to take dramatic action at strategic places. He suggests such possibilities as sit-ins in offices and worship services in buildings of banks that finance apartheid. Such nonviolent actions called for by Kenyatta would not take the place of but would be added to the educational and lobbying work of many organizations, or to mass pro-

---

*"Time to Take Personal Offense," *Engage/Social Action,* December 1981, pp.4–7.

tests like the three thousand person African Liberation Day demonstration in Washington in May 1981. "It is simply meant," he says, "to provide avenues for human beings in this country to witness to our identification with the people of South Africa."

Such witness in the United States would have a much more profound effect on the movement for liberation in South Africa than any arguments for their pursuit of nonviolence that we can make. They seek a radical contribution to their struggle. A strong campaign against United States complicity in the system would be welcome support. If we ask them to consider sacrificial nonviolent struggle, we would best authenticate our call by such actions of our own, limited though they may be.

All of this leads us beyond despair. Indeed we are convinced that hope begins with an honest appraisal of the life that stirs all around us. We do not say that we must complete the American revolution before finding any way to stand in solidarity with those who seek for justice and humane transformation of their society in South Africa or elsewhere. Rather we believe that we are called to both tasks at once, recognizing that they are ultimately one task. And when we look again at South Africa we are encouraged, for we see not only strong evidence of a people's continuing, creative experimentation with nonviolent action—such as the highly effective school boycotts of the last two years, and many of the strikes and other labor actions—but even beyond those important specifics we are ultimately encouraged because we believe that we have also seen the truth of the South African poet Dennis Brutus' affirmation,

> most cruel, all our land is scarred with terror,
> rendered unlovely and unloveable;
> sundered are we and all our passionate surrender,
> but somehow tenderness survives.

That gives us hope: the "tenderness survives," the humanity will not die. We believe, we know, that it is from the heart of such humanity new forms of creative struggle will emerge, for them and for us. It is in the midst of those harsh shadows of death that we see women and men who are determined to create new light, to share that which is already within them. We look at South Africa and remember the song from the freedom struggle of our land: "This little light of mine, I'm goin' to let it shine." And we recall that the song was sung most fervently, most creatively, most hopefully in jails, in the face of dogs and rifle butts, under the clouds of tear gas. In the midst of all that it was sung and the singing never stopped. The tenderness survives.

*Only South Africa herself has the power to avert what is rapidly becoming inevitable by demolishing the whole apparatus of apartheid, setting all her peoples free from captivity to the past and offering her immense talents and energy in the service of the development of the whole continent. I am not optimistic, but I have much faith in the providence of God. That alone seems to stand between us and the void.*

Kenneth Kaunda, *The Riddle of Violence, p. 178.*

# CHAPTER 8

# *Proposals for Action*

. . . the great South African adventure, that intense and special
dialogue between the people and the earth which shapes and
fashions and nurtures them, can only begin when the land is rid of
this racial ugliness. This must be done before there can be any real
beginning.

Peter Abrahams, *A Night of Their Own.* *

Whomever apartheid touches, it damages. The oppressor and the oppressed are in a relationship which stunts the human potential of each. The
damage from apartheid spreads through all of southern Africa in widening
circles of interaction, whether economic ties or political antagonisms. Acts
of warfare are continuous between SWAPO and South Africa on the Namibian border. South Africa carries out sporadic military raids on Angola,
Zambia and Mozambique. The liberation movements resort to acts of urban sabotage. Black and white, South Africans live in fear, a fear which
reaches into neighboring communities and beyond. For Quakers and many
others, apartheid is a denial of God's will.

The United Nations has wrestled extensively with these problems which
are continuously on its agenda. The results are minimal, due primarily to
the South African government's intransigence. But government action is affected by the concern of citizens. It is time for citizens of this country and
other countries to step up their campaigns of education and to tell their
governments and the South African government that basic changes must be
made in South Africa quickly, for delay increases the potential for disaster.
There are many ways to communicate that message. Our proposals for action are ways to commuicate. We urge widespread citizen participation in
relevant action. Apathy supports apartheid.

We need to recognize the extent to which our own lives as Americans are
involved in the South African situation and the extent to which our attitudes
toward South Africa reflect our own racism or complicity with an unjust

---

*New York: Alfred A. Knopf, 1965, p. 220.

system. We must ask ourselves to overcome the fear of losing elements of privilege and control as we work for a more egalitarian society in our country. It would be hypocritical to ask South Africans to relinquish such elements in their own lives and be unwilling to act comparably ourselves. We and South Africans must heed the words of Thomas Merton, writing in the midst of the U.S. civil rights struggle of the sixties: "We must dare to pay the dolorous price of change, *to grow into a new society.* Nothing else will suffice!"*

How can we begin to move? We propose several areas for concerted negotiation and action. We have not tried to list all options but to suggest areas where activity can be significant, where change may be effected and have the possibility of leading to further progress. Each area of action can help create a climate of trust for next steps to avert cataclysmic confrontation. We have included a wide variety of options, so that any individual or group should find some opportunities for action and growth.

## Two Objectives

Specific suggestions for action are listed below. These actions are directed toward two broad objectives.

*To withdraw support from apartheid.*

Apartheid will flourish in direct proportion to its support. As long as there is foreign acceptance of, cooperation with, and financing of apartheid, it will not disappear. Increased pressures to withdraw such support are essential. Our complicity in the iniquitous system must be removed for religious and moral reasons.

*To support South African efforts for change.*

South African efforts to achieve a just and more egalitarian society can be aided by outside support and encouragement. Even as we press for withdrawal of support for the system we deplore, we should be ready to cooperate with and, if possible, participate in the variety of South African efforts for positive social transformation that are consistent with our principles. We favor communicating this positive stance to all South Africans to demonstrate our concern for the quality of life which creative change can bring to all members of the South African society.

## Proposals

*Namibia*

The independence of Namibia is a top priority item for the frontline

---

*Seeds of Destruction* (New York: Farrar, Straus and Giroux, 1965), p. 9.

states, the United Nations, the OAU and the Reagan administration southern Africa policy. The South African government has officially agreed with the people of Namibia and the international community that Namibian independence is a legitimate goal, but Pretoria has constantly frustrated efforts to bring it about.

Namibia has gained this prominence on so many agendas because it is the last colonial area in Africa to gain its independence. Also, guerrilla warfare on the Namibia/Angola border strains the resources of both Angola and Namibia and is costly in human lives. With twenty-five thousand soldiers in the border area, the cost is high for South Africa, too. And since SWAPO is being supported by the Soviet Union and there are Cuban troops in Angola, Namibian independence has become an issue in the East/West conflict.

Namibia is probably the place where the most useful change could be brought the most quickly in southern Africa. Since change must be implemented by governments, we urge the United States government, the South African government and the many other governments working on this problem to move immediately to implementation of UN Resolution 435, to which all of them have agreed in principle. We believe that citizens of the U.S. and other countries should work to see that their governments apply pressure, including sanctions if necessary, on the South African government to reach a long overdue settlement for Namibian independence.

### Southern African States

The dependence of the southern African states on South Africa helps to buttress apartheid. It is evident that these nations have no immediate opportunities for withdrawing from this dependency. Material and financial support from the rest of the world to these countries could have an immediate and important effect on the status quo in South Africa. It is in the long term interest of the whole region to establish cooperative and mutually beneficial relationships, but it is foolish to imagine that such relationships can be fruitful so long as apartheid exists. We propose that the nations of the world offer direct support in the form of financial assistance and goods (agricultural, technological) to the southern African states. Help should be given to the Southern Africa Development Coordination Conference (see page 74), in order to help them accelerate the process of becoming less involved in the South African economy and giving them greater ability to negotiate. Such an action may be undertaken by any group of nations. This aid could become a positive program of the United Nations to help end apartheid.

Support to Zimbabwe may have a special impact on South Africa. Zimbabwe is the country that has most recently changed to majority rule. If South African whites see that the chaos and atrocities they predicted do not materialize, Zimbabwe will provide an example of a positive alternative for their future. Zimbabwe needs and has asked for help to develop economic, social and political strength and to demonstrate the vision of a viable nonracial society. Material and moral support to Zimbabwe both helps that nation withdraw from reliance on South Africa and offers another "beacon of hope" to the people of South Africa. International aid commitments from the U.S. and other nations are encouraging and must be continued as the new nation wrestles with its problems.

### Increased Interaction

Students, black leaders and some white leaders who are committed to changing South African society badly need support from outside. This may be offered in a number of ways. Students need sponsorship in any country where they can study. Since education within South Africa is so inadequate for blacks, ways should be sought to help strengthen the pool of leadership through special courses and scholarships.

Well planned, off-the-record meetings and conferences can involve South Africans in serious discussion for which few present opportunities exist. From such efforts, a new vision and plans for the transition may emerge. We propose that individuals and groups sponsor those who want and need to come out of South Africa, arrange opportunities for South Africans who are out of their country to communicate and plan together, and arrange special forums in which serious dialogue can occur.

Refugees and exiles need special support. They need direct material aid and political asylum. They also need opportunities for dialogue and planning, including training for future leadership roles, for example through the liberation organizations and agencies such as the UN Institute for Namibia, operating in Zambia.

For quite different reasons South Africans need personal relationships in Zimbabwe and the United States, as well as in many other countries. In Zimbabwe they could experience a nonracial African government striving to meet the needs of all its peoples. They need to see that Zimbabwe is different from what most white South Africans expected. In the United States they could experience the ease with which a society can function with open public accomodation. If interested, they could learn about the race problems they will face after apartheid is ended. South Africans have an extremely limited opportunity to know what the rest of the world is like, especially the rest of Africa. There is considerable unreality spawned by their isolation and insulation. Doors need to be opened for fresh experience and new ideas. Communication is needed at many levels, and where possible it should be two-way.

Our belief in the value of two-way communication and the knowledge that access to information is limited in South Africa leads us to offer recommendations about travel to that country. A traveller is filled with ambiguous feelings because of the inevitable complicity with the apartheid system. The government's authority to grant a visa and to regulate one's daily life must be accepted while in South Africa. It will become evident to the visitor that that daily life is filled with apartheid regulations, from the ridiculous and inconvenient to the immoral and infuriating.

We oppose visits to South Africa by those who choose to benefit from the system and its standard of living for whites. We oppose pleasure trips by tourists. We object to visits made by those who can be used by the South African government to support the illusion that South Africa is no different from other countries. Therefore we believe that entertainers and sports figures or teams should not go to South Africa. We protest visits by those seeking to benefit from the exploitative situation in South Africa. Under this category we include those promoting closer trade and business relations within the apartheid system.

As an example of tourism being used for propaganda purposes, Henry Shank made a visit to South Africa and wrote, in part, to the *Wall Street Journal* (April 7, 1981),

> Black settlements in rural and suburban areas compare favorably with housing occupied by blacks in this country. Such places are neat and clean, with gardens, flowers and every evidence of pride in ownership. Certainly there is separatism, but if there are separate hospital entrances, the waiting room I entered was a common one, as was the subsequent attention. Not so different in our country a few years ago, and close up a lot more temperate in practice than we have been led to believe.

Mr. Shanks' letter was quoted at length in *Straight Talk on South Africa* (December 1981), a publication of the South African Ministry of Information. On the front page of the same issue was a picture of the South African Minister of Foreign Affairs, Roelof Botha, chatting with President Reagan in the White House.

On the other hand, we encourage visits made by those who carry a deep moral motivation to identify with and support the forces for change, whose hearts are filled with outrage at a system which denies that of God in most of its population and which incorporates racism in the law as well as the custom of the land. Visitors can share valuable perspectives and information with South Africans whose news sources are restricted. Others may bring needed expertise or assistance to those working for change. Such visitors need to be sure they see and hear a variety of people and so be able to share insights and up-to-date news upon their return. They can develop personal human bonds with South Africans, so critical in this intractable and divisive situation.

People who go to South Africa should be willing to witness to their beliefs if the way opens. If moved by conscience, they should be willing to confront and challenge the system of apartheid. Searching questions should be asked of those who believe in apartheid, those who passively accept and those who challenge it. Love and respect for all people require no less than this kind of honesty.

## Public Education and Action

When AFSC representatives met with Bishop Tutu in 1980 he urged them to continue to inform the American public about South Africa. He emphasized the need for accurate information and analysis in order to challenge the well-financed efforts of the South African government to paint a rosy picture of their country. Tutu realized that few Americans are knowledgeable about South Africa in any way, much less about the complex issues there. Without basic information about the history of South Africa, the realities of apartheid, the aspirations and feelings of all the people, we cannot hope to support changes effectively there. Nor can we do so without access to information about the changing events and relationships in South Africa. Increased interaction contributes to an understanding of conditions in South Africa. But personal experiences need to be reported and expanded to become part of public education campaigns to reach more people. Such campaigns can be focused on the media, on church groups, on schools and universities, on labor groups and on political constituencies. The need for dissemination of information about South Africa is great and is seen by black South Africans as significant support for their struggle.

Education campaigns are probably most effective when linked to issues of concern to people. Links can be made with labor unions about the export of jobs, as well as with a concern for the international labor movement, workers' rights and other issues which are universal. Links can be made with women's groups about the double oppression of women as well as issues of particular concern such as the use of Depo-Provera, a contraceptive considered too questionable for use in the U.S. but distributed in southern Africa. Links can be made with church groups which can learn about, challenge and/or support their sister denominations in South Africa. The strong emphasis on Christianity by apartheid's leaders makes church dialogue on ethical and theological issues particularly important. In other cases, churches in South Africa need support in their opposition to the system. We recommend that public education programs seek and utilize links with issues of concern to particular groups in the U.S.

Public education can also focus effectively on particular campaigns. These can be in direct support of efforts in South Africa. The international campaign to prevent the South African government from destroying Crossroads, a response to a crisis, effectively supported resistance inside South Africa. Other campaigns have longer-range goals, such as the petition to free Nelson Mandela. Public education can lay the foundation for response to crises and become more significant as it provides opportunities for action to those who have learned about South Africa.

Public education must include judgments about changes in South Africa. In previous chapters we discussed the difficulties of bringing about change. Here we offer a few guidelines for the evaluation of proposed changes. Negative answers to the following questions should be a warning to a person who hopes for a fundamental transformation of South African society.

1. Does the change alter basic power relationships?

2. Are blacks who are respected and supported by the majority of people involved in initiating and planning the change?

3. Do diverse groups inside and outside of South Africa voice approval for the change?

4. Are costs paid primarily by those in power and benefits accrued primarily to those without power?

5. Are goals to which the change contributes articulated?

6. Are appropriate means for implementation announced and followed?

7. Is there a timetable for swift, visible achievement of goals?

### Direct Support to South Africans

We recommend specific means for direct support. First, funds can be contributed to organizations which work for fundamental change or in support of the majority of people. While many organizations may be appropriate, we commend two because of their current situations and impact. The first is the South African Council of Churches, which runs many programs and whose staff are among the few critics who can legally speak in South Africa. The South African government has been increasing pressure and restrictions on the SACC, so it needs both financial and moral support. Second, we urge the exploration of ways to contribute to black trade unions in South Africa, which are becoming increasingly effective. Donations might be made to strike funds. An international fund might be fostered to aid families of strikers.

A second means of direct support to those working for fundamental change in South Africa is the provision of technical and human resources. Responses should be made to particular requests by South Africans. It is not the role of outsiders to determine the priorities or approaches for those in South Africa, including unilateral decisions about the most appropriate aid. Offers should be made in consultation with and in response to requests from South Africans.

Donations of money, technology or resources can be offered by individuals, by groups, by governments or by international bodies. We do not suggest that deciding to whom to give aid is simple. Guidelines to evaluate change and the complexities discussed in Chapter 7 should be considered. Dilemmas arising from past AFSC experience described in Chapter 1 also need careful review. Yet efforts can and should be made to offer technical and human resources to support changes toward justice and equality in South Africa.

### Economic Pressures

Many actions are possible in the economic arena from the implementation of employment codes to selective withdrawal to boycotts to complete withdrawal to sanctions. For those corporations which do not withdraw, there are actions that can be promoted at stockholders' meetings which can also serve educational functions. Corporations can humanize conditions for some black South Africans by providing training, improved housing and opportunities for advancement, including training for supervision on a nonracial basis. In a society where full humanity is denied to a majority of the people, actions to affirm that humanity are important.

Corporations can also selectively refuse to participate in the apartheid system. A corporation can challenge the Group Areas Act of Influx Control and Pass Laws by providing family housing for workers near the site of employment. The Rietspruit mine, for example, is jointly owned by Shell Oil Company and the Barlow Rand Company of South Africa. It is unique among South African mines in that it is exempted from the rule that no more than three percent of the African employees can be housed with their families at any mine. A corporation could also refuse to take part in the military and security requirements described in Chapter 5. No corporation should operate in South Africa without conscious efforts to improve the life of blacks and to challenge the apartheid system.

We believe, however, that economic disengagement makes a more significant contribution to fundamental change. To withdraw support from a system is one way to insist on its change. Withdrawal from involvement in the economy of South Africa can be an important factor in creating the climate for change. Withdrawal is a direct message. It communicates that we who withdraw cannot continue to benefit from or help prolong the system of apartheid. Withdrawal also communicates the strong positive message that we look forward to and welcome the time when we may be able to reopen economic relations with South Africa as it creates a just society for all its people. We propose that individuals, groups, corporations and nations withdraw from present involvement in support of the South African economy in order to communicate these clear and direct messages to the people of South Africa.

A personal boycott of South African products provides an educational conversation piece with other consumers and is a personal reminder of our need to continue the search for a creative solution for South Africa. The personal boycott helps remove one from complicity with apartheid and is one more tool of communication.

*Diplomatic Efforts*

Diplomatic relations represent a level of interaction of one nation with another which to many persons implies some mutual acceptance of national policies. In situations where strong ideological or political differences emerge, diplomatic ties have often been broken. However, over the years Friends and others have consistently maintained that the need for human and governmental interchange is greatest in time of crisis and strain and have urged the continuance or reopening of diplomatic channels.

We see the same need now in our dealings with South Africa, but we also recognize and advocate the necessity for some powerful diplomatic statement of our country's disapproval of that government's oppressive policies. For instance, it is possible to maintain relationships while reducing or changing the assignments of diplomatic personnel. The ambassadorship can be left vacant, leaving responsibility to a charge d'affaires. Commercial and military attaches can be replaced by additional labor and cultural attaches. The embassy and consulates can increase their outreach into all segments of the total community. New kinds of diplomatic personnel can be trained as communicators, with significant language skills. No matter what the rank, high ability and commitment are needed from diplomatic representatives.

The United States and other governments should request steps to implement the South Africa government's "reform" pronouncements. The "end of petty apartheid," or of "discriminatory practices," though loudly proclaimed, bring cynicism to blacks who feel no significant change. Laws that may no longer be enforced but are permitted to remain on the books retain their threat from a petty bureaucracy that too often believes in their "necessity."

Specifically, we ask our government to support in any way it can the demands for the repeal of those laws based primarily on race. Among laws meriting special attention are the following: (1) the Group Areas Act, (2) Pass Laws, (3) the Population Registration Act, and (4) the Prohibition of Mixed Marriages Act. The possibility of success for such actions may not be as remote as appears at first glance. The removal of similar racially based laws has already occurred in Namibia. The Afrikaans language newspaper *Rapport* reported in December 1981 a growing popular acceptance by whites of the elimination of some apartheid laws in South Africa.

Sanctions are a tool which, like most tools, can be used well or can be misused. The U.S. application of sanctions has often seemed inappropriate to us. Yet sanctions are mong the nonviolent tools that have often been effective, and we urge the selective use of government sanctions against South Africa. Recent relaxation of sanctions by the Reagan Administration should be reversed, particularly on the sale of high technology equipment. UN sanctions on the other hand, should be supported.

The South African government will no doubt weigh options and, as in the past, take politically possible steps without fundamentally altering the power structure or inviting the participation of the majority of the population in its decision making. This is not enough. The U.S. should challenge South Africa to announce prospective changes in principle together with the steps or stages they propose to use in achieving those goals. Changes which do alter the power structure and involve the participation of the majority should be applauded.


**Conclusion**

The suggestions discussed here may be approached in a variety of ways. Some are more suitable for individuals than for groups. Individuals can, for example, sponsor students and support refugees. Individual actions are transformed and strengthened when joined with others. It is important to involve many people in these actions and the issues behind them in order to change the world climate which allows this unjust system to continue. Some efforts are nongovernmental while others must be focused on U.S. policy and practice. But the racism in our own society is the main reality that supports racist and oppressive regimes elsewhere. We must continue to address this problem.

There are many ways for people to become involved: accelerated public education campaigns, media campaigns, organized efforts to effect particular pieces of legislation, demonstrations, shareholder activities, nonviolent direct action, and many more options for organizing. All of these should be pursued to change the U.S. impact on South Africa.

A prisoner has a single need: to get out. There may be a multitude of problems after release, but the basic one will be solved with freedom. In the system of apartheid, the South African government is both the jailer and the jailed. We call on that government to begin now to free itself, for freedom from apartheid is a process, not a single act. The government talks about many changes it has underway, but the international community is unconvinced. Most important of all, black South Africans are not convinced. We suggest a single substantive act of great symbolic importance to be taken immediately to start the needed process.

We urge the South African government to simply allow African families to live together. This means the end of unisex workers' hostels, a sharp reduction in migratory labor, no more bulldozing of squatter camps, a provision for rapid increase in family residences, including private homes on secure leaseholds, and the end of forced removals and resettlements. It specifically means that normally a spouse and children would be allowed to live with the family wage earner wherever he or she is employed. Family life is a human need too often denied by apartheid.

We support the oppressed of South Africa who are struggling for liberation and we are confident that they will remain steadfast in the cause of justice. We hope that those who struggle will keep on talking to all who will talk and listen. We urge them to remain open to new ideas for movement toward liberation from wherever they may come, including the South African government. We pray that nonviolent, constructive steps will be taken toward alternatives to repression and to violent chaotic revolution. There are spiritual resources to be tapped, but the decision on tactics remains with those struggling for freedom.

We call on our fellow citizens to assume our share of responsibility for South Africa. We ask each one to act to end apartheid.

We end as we began, conscious of our hope, our vision, our responsibility and our shortcomings. We acknowledge that in making proposals to help free South Africa we face an enormous challenge. We need to work to free our own society of the shackles on many of our own fellow citizens. Since there is, in the Quaker expression, "that of God in everyone," no one may be wrongfully denied the chance to be and to live free. The knowledge of our common humanity impels us to seek an end to racism, exploitation and oppression everywhere. Because we know that these conditions exist we must assume responsibility for helping to end them. Only in this way can we be true to our own deepest spiritual commitment. We find hope in the indomitable human spirit to face this challenge and know that there are many ways we can be effective.

Finally, we also appeal to those now in authority in South Africa, who carry heavy and complex burdens of responsibility for all the people who make up their complicated society, to search for a new vision to bring real and all-inclusive security to the total population. The search for alternatives must encompass the wisdom of all segments, not rigidly separated into compartments but fully participating in the common aspirations. God's message for building his Kingdom is not restricted, but finds expression in the rich diversity of His people. His Kingdom is not built with nor maintained by military force but by the love His followers exhibit towards Him and their neighbors. Long ago the prophet Isaiah quoted the Lord:

> If you put an end to oppression, to every gesture of contempt, and to every evil word; if you give food to the hungry and satisfy those who are in need, then the darkness around you will turn to the brightness of noon. And I will always guide you and satisfy you with good things. I will keep you strong and well. You will be like a garden that has plenty of water, like a spring of water that never runs dry. Your people will rebuild what has long been in ruins, building again on old foundations. You will be known as the people who rebuilt the walls, who restored the ruined houses."*

---

*Good News Bible, published worldwide, including South Africa.

# *Chronology*

| | |
|---|---|
| 1652 | First settlement at the Cape of Good Hope by Europeans (Dutch East India Company) |
| 1657 | Dutch East India Company frees a few employees to create the nucleus of settlers |
| 1658 | First substantial importation of slaves |
| 1659–60 | First Khoikhoi–Dutch war |
| 1673–77 | Second Khoikhoi–Dutch war |
| 1688 | Arrival of 200 French Huguenot settlers |
| 1779–81 | First frontier war with Xhosa |
| 1793 | Second frontier war |
| 1795 | First British occupation of the Cape |
| 1799 | Third frontier war |
| 1803 | Cape restored temporarily to Dutch rule |
| 1806 | Second British occupation |
| 1807 | Abolition of the slave trade in the British Empire |
| 1814 | British acquire permanent sovereignty over the Cape |
| 1820 | Arrival of 5,000 British immigrants |
| 1828 | British make English the official language of South Africa |
| 1834 | Beginning of slave emancipation in the British Empire |
| 1834–35 | Major war with Xhosa on the eastern frontier; English and Dutch involved |
| 1836–38 | The Great Trek |
| 1838 | Trekking Boers defeat Zulu at the Battle of Blood River |
| | Founding of the Boer Republic in Natal |
| | Completion of slave emancipation in the Cape Colony |
| 1843 | British annexation of Natal |
| 1848 | British government proclaims its sovereignty between the Orange and Vaal rivers |
| 1852 | British recognize the independence of the Boers in the Transvaal |
| 1854 | British grant independence to the Orange Free State |
| | Cape Colony granted representative government; establishment of nonracial franchise |
| 1858 | Founding of the South African Republic by the Boers in the Transvaal |
| 1860 | Indian indentured laborers introduced into Natal by British |
| 1867 | Discovery of diamonds |
| 1872 | Cape Colony granted responsible, cabinet government |

| 1877 | Annexation of the Transvaal by the British |
| 1879 | British-Zulu war |
| 1880 | First Anglo–Boer war |
| 1881 | Transvaal Republic regains its independence |
| 1884 | First big gold field found in Transvaal |
| 1893 | Natal granted responsible government |
| 1894 | Mahatma Gandhi arrived in South Africa |
|      | Natal Indian Congress formed |
| 1895 | The Jameson raid (abortive attempt by pro-British to overthrow the Transvaal government) |
| 1899 | Outbreak of the second Anglo--Boer war |
| 1902 | End of Anglo–Boer war (called Second War of Freedom by Afrikaners) |
|      | Peace of Vereeniging |
| 1905 | South African Native Affairs Commission advocates territorial segregation of whites and Africans |
| 1906 | Gandhi coined word *Satyagraha* (force which is born of truth and love) |
|      | Zulu rebellion in Natal |
| 1907 | Cape Colony School Board Act restricts access of nonwhites to public education |
|      | Attainment of responsible government by the Transvaal and the Orange Free State |
|      | Asiatic Registration Act passed by Transvaal |
|      | Gandhi-led resistance campaign begins |
| 1909 | South African Native Convention met, asked extension of Cape Franchise and end of color bar |
| 1910 | Establishment of the Union of South Africa |
| 1911 | Mine and Works Act of Union Parliament sanctions an industrial color bar |
|      | Strikes by Africans made a crime |
| 1912 | African National Congress founded |
| 1913 | Native Land Act prohibits Africans from buying land outside of reserves |
| 1915 | Mahatma Gandhi leads march of over 2,000 Indians into Transvaal, courting arrest |
| 1919 | ANC anti-pass campaign, 700 arrests in Johannesburg |
|      | 400 dockworkers strike in Cape Town |
| 1920 | South West Africa mandated to South Africa by the League of Nations |

| 1926 | Colour Bar Act secures a monopoly on skilled jobs for white mineworkers |
|---|---|
| | South African Indian Congress formed |
| 1930 | White women enfranchised |
| | Three blacks killed by police at pass-burning demonstration |
| 1931 | Statute of Westminister |
| 1932 | African women organize passive resistance against curfew regulations in Transvaal |
| 1934 | Founding of Purified National Party by Afrikaner opponents of Hertzog's coalition |
| 1936 | Africans removed from the common voters' role in the Cape Province |
| 1943 | Alexandra bus boycott |
| | African Mineworkers Union strike involves 73,557 workers; 9 killed by police |
| 1944 | 600 Indians jailed in Natal passive resistance against segregation |
| | Congress Youth League formed |
| 1945 | Dr. A. B. Zuma publishes *African Claims,* applying Atlantic Charter ideals to South Africa |
| 1946 | African mineworkers' strike broken by police |
| | Nearly 2,000 Indians (and a few whites, including Rev. Michael Scott) jailed in Natal for nonviolent resistance to anti-Indian legislation |
| | UN General Assembly denies South Africa request to annex South West Africa |
| 1948 | National Party victory over the United Party in parliamentary elections |
| 1949 | Prohibition of Mixed Marriages Act |
| | Population Registration Act |
| | ANC Youth League calls for civil disobedience and non-cooperation against pass law and apartheid |
| 1950 | Group Areas Act |
| | Police fire on mass labor strike in Transvaal, 18 blacks killed |
| | Communist Party made unlawful |
| 1951 | Bantu Authorities Act establishes a new system of government for African reserves |
| 1952 | ANC and Indian Congress deliberately break segregation laws in the Campaign Against Unjust Laws |
| | 8,000 arrested nationwide, 14 killed by police, 35 wounded |

| 1953 | Reservation of Separate Amenities Act |
| | Bantu Education Act |
| 1954 | World Council of Churches makes strong statement against racism without dissent |
| 1955 | 10,000 children stay out of school in Bantu Education Act protest |
| | Freedom Charter adopted |
| 1956 | Thousands of African women protest pass laws, 3 killed by police |
| | Coloureds removed from common voters' roll in Cape Province |
| | Treason trial of 156 persons |
| 1959 | Pan Africanist Congress formed by Robert Sobukwe |
| 1960 | A.J. Luthuli wins Nobel Peace Prize |
| | SWAPO organized |
| | Sharpeville Massacre |
| | Cottesloe ecumenical consultation |
| | PAC and ANC banned |
| 1961 | South Africa becomes a republic and severs ties with the British Commonwealth |
| | ANC organizes Umkonto We Sizwe (Spear of the Nation) |
| 1963 | Organization of African Unity founded |
| | Nelson Mandela and Walter Sisulu sentenced to life in prison under the Suppression of Communism Act |
| 1964 | Malawi becomes independent |
| | Zambia becomes independent |
| 1966 | Herman Toivo ja Toivo, SWAPO founder, sentenced to 20 years in prison |
| | Botswana becomes independent |
| | Lesotho becomes independent |
| 1968 | Creation of Coloured Persons' Representative Council (terminated 1980) |
| | Swaziland becomes independent |
| 1969 | Steve Biko elected first president of South African Students' Organization (SASO) |
| 1970 | UN Security Council Resolution 283 calls on all countries to end economic involvement of their nationals in Namibia |
| | First World Council of Churches grant for humanitarian needs of southern Africa liberation movements |
| 1971 | African workers strike in Namibia and win minor concessions |
| | World Council of Churches withdraws invested funds from corporations operating in South Africa |

| 1972 | Black dockworkers strike in Durban and win pay increase. |
|------|------|
| 1973 | First British Council of Churches study on investment in South Africa |
| | UN General Assembly declares SWAPO to be "sole authentic representative of the people of Namibia" |
| | 70,000 strike in Durban, Cape Town and Hammersdale |
| 1975 | Mozambique becomes independent |
| | Angola becomes independent |
| 1976 | Soweto uprising, protests spread across country, over 1,000 killed |
| | Transkei declared independent by South Africa |
| 1977 | Steve Biko killed while in police custody |
| | UN approves mandatory arms embargo against South Africa |
| | 17 Black Consciousness organizations and the Christian Institute declared unlawful |
| | Bophuthatswana declared independent by South Africa |
| 1978 | Azanian People's Organization (AZAPO), a Black Consciousness group, organized |
| | UN Security Council endorses Resolution 435 as Namibian Settlement Plan |
| 1979 | British Council of Churches calls for economic disengagement from South Africa and an international oil boycott |
| | Bantu Education Act replaced by Education and Training Act#90 |
| | Venda declared independent by South Africa |
| 1980 | Zimbabwe becomes independent |
| 1981 | Geneva conference on Namibia fails to reach agreement |
| | National Party wins new election but with loss of votes to both liberals and conservatives |
| | Ciskei declared independent by South Africa |
| 1982 | UN General Assembly proclaimed 1982 as the International Year of Mobilization for Sanctions against South Africa |
| | National Party in South Africa splits, with formation of rightwing Conservative Party of South Africa |

# *Appendix*

## Abbreviations

| | |
|---|---|
| AFSC | American Friends Service Committee |
| APO | African Political Organization |
| ANC | African National Congress |
| ARMSCOR | Armaments Development and Production Company |
| AZAPO | Azanian People's Organization |
| BCP | Black Community Programs |
| BCC | British Council of Churches |
| BCM | Black Consciousness Movement |
| BPC | Black People's Convention |
| DRC | Dutch Reformed Church |
| DTA | Democratic Turnhalle Alliance |
| EEC | European Economic Community |
| ESCOM | Electricity Supply Commission |
| FRELIMO | Front for Liberation of Mozambique |
| ISCOR | South African Iron and Steel Industrial Corporation |
| MPLA | Popular Movement for the Liberation of Angola |
| NUSAS | National Union of South African Students |
| OAU | Organization of African Unity |
| PAC | Pan Africanist Congress |
| QPS | Quaker Peace and Service (formerly Friends Service Council) |
| SABC | South African Broadcasting Corporation |
| SACC | South African Council of Churches |
| SAIRR | South African Institute of Race Relations |
| SAR&H | South African Railways and Harbors |
| SASM | South African Student Movement |
| SASO | South African Student Organization |
| SASOL | South African Coal, Oil and Gas Corporation |
| SAYM | Southern African Yearly Meeting of Friends (Quakers) |
| SOWETO | South West Townships |
| SWAPO | South West African People's Organization |
| UDI | Unilateral Declaration of Independence |
| UN | United Nations |
| UNITA | National Union for the Total Independence of Angola |
| USSALEP | U.S.-South Africa Leader Exchange Program |
| WCC | World Council of Churches |
| ZANU-PF | Zimbabwe National Union (Patriotic Front) |
| ZAPU | Zimbabwe African People's Union |

# Glossary

African National Congress (ANC)—South African liberation movement.

Africans—Used in this document for black ethnic groups originating in Africa. Most Afrikaners consider themselves to be white Africans.

Afrikaners—White persons of Dutch/Huguenot ancestry whose first language is Afrikaans and who first immigrated to South Africa in the seventeenth century.

Amandla Ngawethu!—Zulu for "Power is ours!"

Angola—Former Portuguese territory. Independent in 1975.

Apartheid—The South African economic, political and social system based on race, "separateness."

Azania—Name used by PAC and Black Consciousness organizations for South Africa. ANC does not use this name.

Azanian People's Organization (AZAPO)—Black consciousness group, presently (August 1982) legal and operating in South Africa.

Bantu—Word used in South Africa synonomous with African, disliked by blacks. Properly refers to an African linguistic group.

Bantu Education Act—Law on African education from 1953 to 1979. Designed to educate Africans for their "proper place."

Bantustan—Early name for areas now called homelands.

Biko, Steve—First president of South Africans Student Organization, a leader of Black Consciousness Movement.

Black Consciousness Movement—South African black power movement, crosses African political and ethnic lines.

Blacks—Usually means Africans, Indians and coloured. Sometime refers only to Africans.

Black Sash—Organization of predominantly white women who wear black sashes in their frequent demonstrations against the impact of apartheid.

Boers—First designation of group now called Afrikaners. Literally in Dutch, "farmers."

Botha, P.W.—Prime Minister of South Africa.*

Botha, R.F. "Pik"—Minister of Foreign Affairs for South Africa.*

Botswana—Former British Protectorate called Bechuanaland. Independent 1966.

Broederbond—Secret society of Afrikaner leaders, a behind-the-scenes power center.

Brutus, Dennis—Black South African poet, a political exile in the U.S.

Cape Province—One of four provinces of South Africa.

Christian Institute—Interracial, ecumenical organization founded by Rev. Beyers Naude to work against apartheid. Banned, October 1977.

Coloureds (Coloreds)—Persons of mixed race ancestry. The majority have Afrikaans as a first language.

Congress Youth League—Youth section of ANC, founded 1943.

---

*Office held at time of publication.

Conservative Party of South Africa—New party formed in 1982 in rightwing split from National Party.

Contact Group—United States, United Kingdom, France, Canada, West Germany. Group working on resolution of issues between SWAPO and South Africa for independence of Namibia.

Cottesloe—Ecumenical South African consultation on racism in 1960 called by WCC subsequent to Sharpeville. (Named after place of meeting.)

Crocker, Chester—U.S. Assistant Secretary of State for African Affairs.*

Crossroads—African squatter community outside Cape Town.

Democratic Turnhalle Alliance—Coalition of Namibian political parties in office under South African internal settlement, dominated by whites.

Education and Training Act No. 90—Replacement in 1979 for the Bantu Education Act.

Freedom Charter—Adopted by the Congress of the People (a coalition of ANC and other organizations), in 1955 stating African aspirations for a nonracial, egalitarian state for South Africa.

Front for the Liberation of Mozambique (FRELIMO)—Ruling party in Mozambique.

Frontline States—Originally included states bordering on Zimbabwe except South Africa, plus Angola and Tanzania. Now loosely applied to all states of southern Africa, plus Tanzania, as frontline to South Africa.

Group Areas Act—South African law which segregates areas by race.

Herstigte Nasionale Party—Rightwing Afrikaner political party with no seats in Parliament as of 1981 general election.

Homelands—South African government designation of rural area reserved for Africans according to ethnic groups.

Influx control—System designed to keep unemployed Africans out of South African cities, largely dependent on pass laws.

Kaunda, Dr. Kenneth—President of Zambia.*

Khoikhoi—African ethnic group often called Hottentots; inhabited Cape Province area in the seventeenth century.

Kirkpatrick, Jeane—U.S. Ambassador to the UN.*

Lesotho—Former British Protectorate of Basutoland. Independent 1966.

Luthuli, Chief Albert (1898ca.-1967)—African nationalist leader, deposed from chiefdom by South African government, head of ANC for 10 years. Won Nobel Peace Prize in 1960 in recognition of his leadership in nonviolent struggle for justice.

Machel, Samora—President of Mozambique.* Leader of FRELIMO.

Malawi—Former British territory of Nyasaland. Independent 1964.

Mandela, Nelson—President of ANC serving life prison sentence on Robben Island.*

Mandela, Winnie—ANC leader who has been banned for more than 20 years.

Moose, Richard—U.S. Assistant Secretary of State for African Affairs in the Carter Administration.

Motlana, Dr. Ntatho—Leader of Soweto Committee of 10.

Mozambique—Former Portuguese territory. Independent 1975.

---

*Office held at time of publication.

Mugabe, Robert—Prime Minister of Zimbabwe.* Leader of ZANU-PF.

Namibia—Generally accepted name for former German territory of South West Africa.

Natal—One of four provinces of South Africa.

National Party—Party in power in South Africa. Founded by and controlled by Afrikaners but with participation by other whites. Split 1982.

National Union for the Total Independence of Angola (UNITA)—Guerrilla group contesting for power in Angola.

National Union of South African Students (NUSAS)—A nonracial organization of college students led by English-speaking whites from which SASO split.

Naude, Beyers—Dutch Reformed minister, now banned, who founded the Christian Institute to protest apartheid.

New Conservative Party—Rightwing political party in South Africa with no seats in Parliament as of 1981 general election; merged into the Conservative Party of South Africa in 1982.

New Republic Party—Minor South African political party with 8 seats in Parliament as of 1981 general election. A "center" group between the National Party and the Progressive Federal Party.

Nujoma, Sam—President of SWAPO.*

Nyerere, Julius—President of Tanzania.*

Nzo, Alfred—Secretary General of ANC.*

Orange Free State—one of four provinces of South Africa.

Organization of African Unity (OAU)—Continental association of independent African states, founded in 1963.

Ovambo—Largest ethnic group in Namibia.

Pan Africanist Congress—South African liberation movement founded in 1959. Robert Sobukwe first president.

Parastatals—Corporations controlled by the South African government.

Pass, Passbook (Reference book)—Document required of all adult Africans, includes work history, history of places of residence, permission for presence in area.

Population Registration Act—Law requiring classification of all South Africans by race.

Popular Movement for the Liberation of Angola (MPLA)—Political party in power in Angola.

Program to Combat Racism—Section of World Council of Churches which made grants from special funds to southern African liberations movements for humanitarian purposes.

Progressive Federal Party—Political party in South Africa combining the former Progressive Party and the liberal elements of the United Party. The official opposition.

Prohibition of Political Interference Act—South African law prohibiting interracial membership in political parties.

Quaker Peace and Service (formerly Friends Service Council)—International service agency of London and Ireland Yearly Meetings.

Rand—Unit of South African currency. Equal to $1.00 U.S. early 1982.

---

*Office held at the time of publication.

Republican Front—Post-independence name of the Rhodesian Front, Zimbabwe political party.

Reserves—An early name for bantustans or homelands, still has some usage.

Rhodes, Cecil—British pioneer who opened up territory in central Africa for the British Empire, founder of Rhodesia. Born 1853, died 1902.

Rhodesian Front—Party in power in Rhodesia during the Unilateral Declaration of Independence. Led by Ian Smith.

Robben Island—Maximum security prison for political prisoners. In bay near Cape Town.

San—African ethnic group often called Bushmen; inhabited Cape Province area in the seventeenth century.

dos Santos, Jose Eduardo—President of Angola.*

Savimbi, Jonas—Leader of UNITA.*

Scott, Michael—Anglican clergyman active against apartheid in South Africa for many years. Now retired in England.

Slabbert, Frederik van zyl—Leader of Progressive Federal Party.*

Smith, Ian—Leader of Rhodesian Front, now Republican Front.*

Sobukwe, Robert—Founder of Pan Africanist Congress. Died 1978.

Sotho—One of three largest African ethnic groups in South Africa.

South African Digest—Publication of South African Information Department.

South African Institute of Race Relations—Voluntary organization with headquarters in Johannesburg, good reputation for research of factual information on South Africa. Works to improve race relations in South Africa.

South West African People's Organization (SWAPO)—Liberation movement for Namibia, recognized by UN as representative of Namibian people.

South African Student Movement (SASM)—An activist Black Consciousness organization of high school students.

South African Students Organization (SASO)—Organization of black university students.

South West Africa—Namibia.

Soweto—African township outside of Johannesburg (South West Townships).

Soweto Committee of 10—A leadership group expressing African aspirations which grew out of the 1976 Soweto uprising.

Sullivan, Leon—Baptist minister in Philadelphia, member of the Board of Directors of General Motors, initiator of the Sullivan Principles.*

Survey of Race Relations—Annual report of data by the South African Institute of Race Relations.

Swaziland—Former British Protectorate. Independent 1968.

Tambo, Oliver—President of ANC.*

Tanzania—East African country, active on southern African issues, formed from union of former territories of Tanganyika and Zanzibar in 1964.

Transkei—First African homeland in South Africa given nominal independence.

Transvaal—One of four provinces of South Africa.

---

*Office held at time of publication.

Tutu, Rt. Rev. Desmond—General Secretary of the South African Council of Churches.*

Unilateral Declaration of Independence (UDI)—Rhodesian declaration of independence by Ian Smith, then Prime Minister, 1965.

United National Independence Party (UNIP)—Ruling party in Zambia.

Union of South Africa—Former name (1910–1961) of Republic of South Africa.

Xhosa—One of three largest African ethnic groups in South Africa.

Xuma, Dr. A.B.—Early leader of ANC.

Zambia—Former British territory of Northern Rhodesia. Independent 1964.

Zimbabwe—Formerly called Southern Rhodesia, Rhodesia and Rhodesia-Zimbabwe. Independent 1980.

Zimbabwe African National Union (Patriotic Front) (ZANU–PF)—Ruling party in Zimbabwe.

Zulu—One of three largest African ethnic groups in South Africa.

*Office held at time of publication.

144

# Selected References

Abahams, Peter, *A Night of Their Own,* New York: Alfred A. Knopf, 1965

*Africa News,* Durham, North Carolina, numerous issues

American Friends Service Committee, *Namibia,* Philadelphia, 1981

Bacon, Margaret Hope, *Lucretia Mott Speaking,* Pendle Hill Pamphlet #234, Wallingford, Pa.: Pendle Hill Publications, 1980

Becker, Peter, *Dingane: King of the Zulu 1828-1840,* New York: Thomas Y. Crowell, 1965

Becker, Peter, *Path of Blood: The Rise and Conquests of Mzilikazi, Founder of the Matabele,* Longman, Great Britain, 1962

British Council of Churches, *Political Change in South Africa: Britain's Responsibility,* London, 1979

Brutus, Dennis, *A Simple Lust,* New York: Farrar, Straus and Giroux, 1973

Carter, Gwendolen, *Which Way Is South Africa Going?* Bloomington, Ind.: Indiana University Press, 1980

Foner, Philip S., Ed., *The Life and Writings of Frederick Douglass,* New York: International Publishers, 1950

Fugard, Athol; Kani, John and Ntshona, Winston, *Siswe Bansi is Dead* and *The Island,* New York: The Viking Press, 1973

Gandhi, M. K., *Satyagraha in South Africa,* Academic Reprints, Stanford, California, 1954

Gordon, Loraine, Ed., *Survey of Race Relations in South Africa 1980,* Natal Witness for South African Institute of Race Relations, Johannesburg, South Africa, 1981

Hope, Marjorie and Young, James, *South African Churches in a Revolutionary Situation,* Maryknoll, N.Y.: Orbis Books, 1981

International Institute for Strategic Studies, *The Military Balance 1972-73,* London, 1972

Kaunda, Kenneth, *The Riddle of Violence,* San Francisco: Harper and Row, 1980

Lewin, Julius, *Political and Law in South Africa: Essays on Race Relations,* London: Merlin Press, 1963

Luthuli, Albert, *Let My People Go: The Autobiography of a Great African Leader,* Johannesburg: Collins, 1962

Merton, Thomas, *Seeds of Destruction,* New York: Farrar, Straus and Giroux, 1965

Minogue, Martin and Molloy, Judith, Eds., *African Aims and Attitudes: Selected Documents,* London: Cambridge University Press, 1974

Nash, Margaret, *Black Uprooting from "White" South Africa, The Fourth and Final Stage of Apartheid,* Braamfontein: South African Council of Churches, 1980

Neame, L.E., *The History of Apartheid,* London: Pall Mall Press with Barrie and Rockliff, 1962

Nielson, Waldemar A., *African Battleground, American Policy Choices in South Africa,* New York: Harper and Row for Council on Foreign Relations, 1965

Paton, Alan, *Hope for South Africa,* New York: Praeger, 1959

Rotberg, Robert I., *Suffer the Future: Policy Choices in Southern Africa,* Cambridge, Mass.: Harvard University Press, 1980

Seidman, Judy, *Ba Ye Zwa, The People Live; South Africa: Daily Life Under Apartheid,* Boston: South End Press, 1978

South African Institute of Race Relations, *Race Relations News,* numerous issues, and *Survey of Race Relations in South Africa,* 1980

South African Ministry of Information, *Backgrounder Reports,* numerous issues

South African Ministry of Information, *South Africa Digest,* numerous issues

Study Commission on U.S. Policy Toward Southern Africa, *South Africa: Time Running Out,* New York: University of California Press for Foreign Policy Study Foundation, 1971

Thompson, Leonard and Wilson, Monica, *The Oxford History of South Africa,* Oxford: The Clarendon Press, 1971

Volman, Daniel, *A Continent Besieged: Foreign Military Activities in Africa,* Washington: Institute of Policy Studies Report, 1980

Wiseman, Henry and Taylor, Alastair M., *From Rhodesia to Zimbabwe: The Politics of Transition,* New York: Pergamon Press, 1981

Woods, Donald, *Biko,* London: Paddington Press, 1978

Woods, Donald, *Asking for Trouble,* New York: Atheneum, 1981

Wilkins, Ivor and Strydom, Hans, *Broederbond: The Super-Afrikaners,* London: Transworld Publishers, Ltd., 1979